# Tarahumara

## WHERE NIGHT
## IS THE DAY OF THE MOON

*by Bernard L. Fontana with photographs by John P. Schaefer*

*Second Edition, With a New Preface*

The University of Arizona Press / Tucson

Publication of this book is made possible in part by the
proceeds of a permanent endowment created with the
assistance of a Challenge Grant from the National
Endowment for the Humanities, a federal agency.

The University of Arizona Press
Copyright © 1997
The Arizona Board of Regents

⊗ This book is printed on acid-free,
archival-quality paper.
Manufactured in the United States of America
02  01  00  99  98  97    6  5  4  3  2  1

Library of Congress Cataloging-in-Publication Data
Fontana, Bernard L.
Tarahumara : where night is the day of the moon / Bernard L.
Fontana : with photographs by John P. Schaefer. — 2nd ed., with a new pref.
p.    cm.
Includes bibliographical references and index.
ISBN 0-8165-1706-1 (paper : alk. paper)
1. Tarahumara Indians—Social life and customs.   2. Tarahumara
Indians—Rites and ceremonies.   3. Copper Canyon (Mexico)—Social
life and customs.   I. Schaefer, John Paul, 1934–    .  II. Title.
F1221.T5F66   1997
972'.1049745—dc21   96-29939
CIP

British Library Cataloguing-in-Publication Data
A catalogue record for this book is available from the British Library.

Frontispiece: Felipe Parra
Cover: Maria Serafina and her nephew, Parisio.

# Tarahumara

*For Ralph and Jacquie,*
*who, each year this book was being written,*
*provided a life-renewing haven*

# CONTENTS

# ILLUSTRATIONS

# ACKNOWLEDGMENTS

WE WISH ABOVE ALL to thank Helen Murphey for her generous help through the John and Helen Murphey Foundation. In spirit, at least, she has been with us on all our trips to the Mexican hinterlands. We also wish to thank Edmond Faubert, Clyde Bornhurst, Alexander Russell, Jr., Jean Russell, William Merrill, Father Luis Verplancken, Carmen Gonzáles, and Jaime Aguilar, all of whom helped in ways both large and small. Further, we are indebted to the Polaroid Corporation for the use of their SX-70 camera and color film, the perfect entree to Tarahumara communities. James Enyeart of the Center for Creative Photography at the University of Arizona helped in the selection of photographs to be published; we had hundreds from which to choose.

Finally, we wish to thank our patient wives, Hazel Fontana and Helen Schaefer, and our respective families who tolerated our absences in the Sierra Tarahumara, at the typewriter, and in the darkroom. Not to forget the Rarámuri, who taught us many things about the values of life we had not known before. We hope the Rarámuri who see this book will like it.

B. L. F.
J. P. S.

# TARAHUMARA COUNTRY

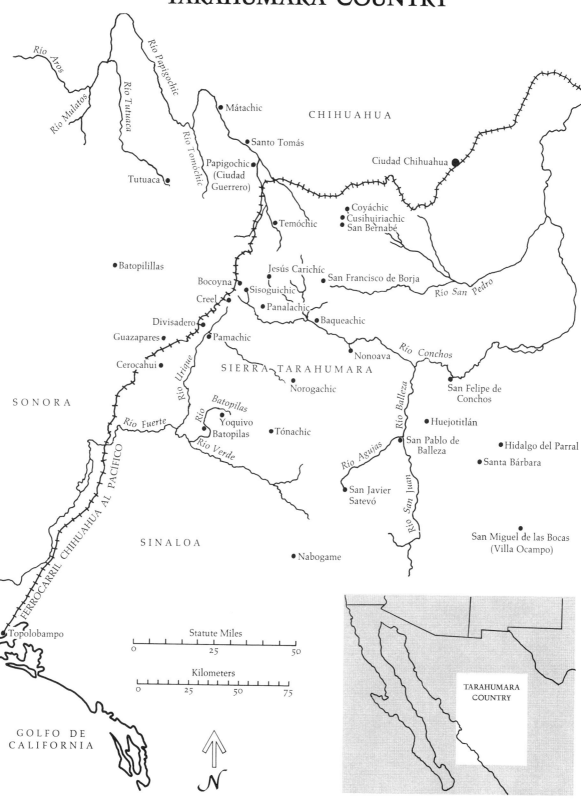

Río Aros
Río Mulatos
Río Papigochic
Río Tutuaca
Río Tomóchic

• Mátachic

CHIHUAHUA

• Santo Tomás

Papigochic
(Ciudad
Guerrero)

Ciudad Chihuahua ●

• Tutuaca

• Coyáchic
• Cusihuiriachic
• San Bernabé

• Temóchic

• Batopilillas

Jesús Carichíc

• San Francisco de Borja

Bocoyna
Creel

• Sisoguichic

Río San Pedro

• Panalachic

Divisadero

• Baqueachic

Guazapares

• Pamachic

Río Conchos

Cerocahui

SIERRA TARAHUMARA

Río Urique

• Nonoava

• San Felipe de
Conchos

SONORA

Batopilas

Norogachic

Río Balleza

Río Fuerte

Río

• Yoquivo
Batopilas

• Huejotitlán

Río Verde

• Tónachic

• Hidalgo del Parral

San Pablo de
Balleza

Río Agujas

Río San Juan

• Santa Bárbara

FERROCARRIL CHIHUAHUA AL PACÍFICO

SINALOA

• San Javier
Satevó

San Miguel de las Bocas
(Villa Ocampo)

• Nabogame

• Topolobampo

Statute Miles

0      25      50

Kilometers

0   25   50   75

GOLFO DE
CALIFORNIA

N

TARAHUMARA
COUNTRY

# PREFACE TO THE
# SECOND EDITION

NEARLY TWO DECADES have gone by since John Schaefer and I last ventured into Tarahumara country. As I walk eastward each morning to pick up the newspaper tossed at the end of the long driveway of my house in the desert south of Tucson, I look wistfully toward the southeast and think how fine it would be to return to that wonderful mountain and canyon domain. Experiences among the Rarámuri inevitably become indelible, and happily so.

To some extent, it has been possible to stay in touch with the Rarámuri through contact with friends who continue regularly to visit or otherwise to deal with these remarkable people. And while the view is undoubtedly distorted, it has been possible for me to remain somewhat abreast of current events in the Sierra Tarahumara through newspaper, magazine, and other published accounts, some of them surely exaggerated and sensationalized to make better copy. What one reads is that the *narcotraficantes* (the growers and distributors of marijuana, opium, and various opium derivatives) have made serious inroads in some parts of Tarahumara country—threatening, intimidating, or cajoling its native inhabitants into cooperating with the international drug trade. The extent to which this is happening is impossible to judge, but whatever its extent it must be laid to the culpability of consumers—and laws—in the United States. We, not they, are the root of the problem.

It is certainly true that the Tarahumaras' semisubsistence economy remains tied to the whims of nature. Episodes of drought and the resulting failed corn crops can produce severe malnutrition and even starvation. Such events have occurred in the years since we last visited them.

It is also true that more roads have been built in the Sierra Tarahumara, many of them paved, and that travel in the Rarámuri's domain has become increasingly less arduous to outsiders. As of July 1996 there were reports that passenger service might be discontinued on the Ferrocarril Chihuahua al Pacífico and, indeed, that the entire railroad operation might cease. But so have there been rumored plans to entice even more tourists into the Chihuahuan mountains over an improved highway network and to have them stay in resortlike accommodations yet to be constructed.

Another verity is that many of the Sierra Tarahumara's remaining forest reserves are under threat of being logged out of existence. Should this occur, the effects on the region's ecology—to say nothing of its inhabitants, Rarámuri and Mexican alike—would be disastrous. It has always been the case that short-term gains carry with them long-term consequences. On the other hand, people who are hungry need more than homilies about the future to allay the immediate longing in their stomachs.

After the text of this book was written and its photographs were selected, the author made two additional trips and the photographer one more visit, this time to the Río Batopilas on the Pacific side of the Continental Divide. The Rarámuri living there showed themselves to be considerably more diffident than those who live to the east. In the depths of this western canyon we were able to visit the incredible eighteenth-century church of the mission of Satevó and to get a sense of Sierra Tarahumara mining history. During the colonial period, the Rarámuri who lived here were conscripted to labor in the mines of New Spain, and in the nineteenth century, when they were employed as laborers working for English and American firms, their situation was probably not much improved. It is not surprising that the Rarámuri who continue to live in this region prefer to deal with outsiders as little as possible except on their own terms.

Countless articles and a few books on the Tarahumaras have appeared since this volume was first published in 1979. Three studies in particular should be added to the list of basic sources in the selected bibliography. These are the most recent version of John G. Kennedy's *Tarahumara of the Sierra Madre* (Pacific Grove, Calif.: Asilomar Press, 1996); William L. Merrill's *Rarámuri Souls: Knowledge and Social Process in Northern Mexico* (Washington, D.C.: Smithsonian Institution Press, 1988); and the book by W. Dirk Raat with photographs by George R. Janeček, *Mexico's Sierra Tarahumara: A Photohistory of the People of the Edge* (Norman: University of Oklahoma Press, 1996). The region of Tarahumara country explored in *Mexico's Sierra Tarahumara* is to the west of the Continental Divide rather than to the east, as in the present volume. Thus our two books are complementary.

The text and photographs in this collaborative effort by John Schaefer and me remain remarkably up-to-date, which, I think, says something about the strength and innate goodness of Rarámuri culture.

BERNARD L. FONTANA
*Tucson, Arizona*

# PREFACE

THEY CALL THEM the Mother Mountains of the West. They are the Sierra Madre Occidental of Mexico. Their towering summits gather in the clouds; their slopes send water rushing over precipitous cliffs and down deep and wide canyons to waiting fields below. In the direction of the sunset their streams and rivers feed the rich agricultural plains of northern Sinaloa and central and southern Sonora, the bread baskets of the nation. To the east the water finds its downward way to the fertile farms of Hidalgo del Parral and Ciudad Chihuahua before continuing an ocean-bound odyssey via the Rio Grande or, as the Mexicans insist, the Río Bravo.

A small portion of this great mountain wall of northwestern Mexico, a mere 20,000 square miles or so—larger than the combined areas of Vermont, Massachusetts, and New Jersey or more than a sixth the size of Arizona—is known locally as the Sierra Tarahumara. Sometimes it is abbreviated simply "Tarahumara." It is a place whose native inhabitants believe that night, death, and the soul are opposite the living in all ways. The spirits of dead people plant in the winter and harvest in March. The soul, manifested in dreams, works at night while the body sleeps. Night is the day of the moon, and it is during this day that spirits of the dead and one's soul move in their mysterious ways. Thus it is that the Tarahumara is where night is the day of the moon, a time for man to sleep and his soul to awaken.

The native inhabitants who hold such beliefs are the Rarámuri or, as that term has come to be mouthed in the words of foreigners, the Tarahumara. In the language of the people it means "foot runners," and it is a properly descriptive term. Almost as soon as they learn to walk, Tarahumara children learn to run. Since time immemorial the most efficient mode of transportation in their mountain fastness, where peaks are higher than 9,000 feet above sea level and where the bottoms of wide canyons known as *barrancas* are below 2,000 feet in altitude, has been by foot. Even today roads are few and far between, and horses, mules, and burros are inefficient when one measures the cost of their upkeep against the benefits. So Tarahumaras continue to walk. And to run.

This book is meant to provide an appreciation, in photographs and words, of these beautiful and gentle people. In all there are possibly 50,000 of them; the mountains and barrancas of the southwestern region of the Mexican State of Chihuahua are their home. The northern perimeters of their territory are fewer than 300 airlines miles south of El Paso, Texas, and fewer than 400 airline miles southeast of Tucson, Arizona. That so many men, women, and children persist in distinctive, centuries-old cultural traditions in spite of their nearness to all the complexities and attractions of modern industrial society is an important part of the story.

What this volume most certainly is not meant to be is a scientific "study" of the Tarahumara. It is based on a very few visits, of all too brief duration, by B. L. Fontana and John Schaefer, both together and independently. All of our trips were in small planes piloted either by Larry Bornhurst or by Alexander Russell, Jr. We were always accompanied by Edmond J. B. Faubert, a man who has traded with Tarahumaras for many years and who was our interpreter both in Spanish and in Tarahumara. It was partially Faubert's introduction of us to people he had known for a long time that made it possible for us to feel quickly at home in alien surroundings. This fact, coupled with extensive reading in the fairly voluminous historical, anthropological, botanical, and medical literature concerning the Tarahumara, perhaps sets us slightly apart from the more usual tourist or casual visitor. We spent a little time in communities that can be reached only by plane or on foot or horseback; we ate the food Tarahumaras themselves eat; in small ways we shared with them the routine of their everyday lives.

It should further be pointed out that all of our time was spent in the upland country of the Sierra Tarahumara, above 6,000 feet, and most of that on the eastern side of the Continental Divide. We did not visit people living in the barrancas or who migrate seasonally from the pine and oak highlands to canyon bottoms. Neither did we become acquainted with many of the presumably more acculturated Tarahumaras who live in centers of immediate Jesuit mission influence and in lumber or mining towns. It is clear from what has already been written about these people, however, that although there are regional differences in food, clothing, houses, and in other artifacts, and while people have been differentially influenced by the "outside world," there is still remarkable underlying consistency in Tarahumara behavior and life-style. Their culture is very much intact.

We have come away with a sense not of, "Who are they?" But rather of, "who are we?" To try to understand the Tarahumara brings one to wonder less about them and more about those of us who would find ways to bring about changes in their lives.

BERNARD L. FONTANA
JOHN P. SCHAEFER
*The University of Arizona*
*Tucson*

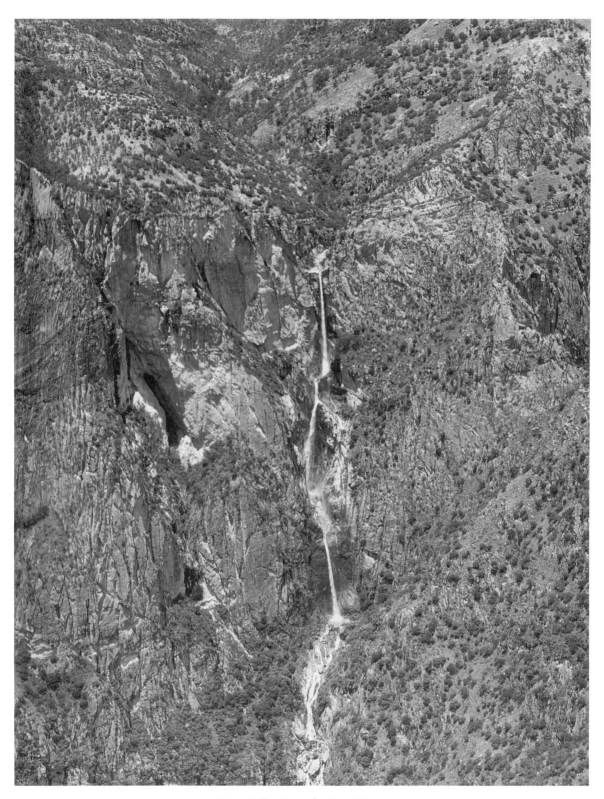

*Waterfalls above the Río Urique*

# CHAPTER ONE

*I cannot say with certitude what the distance is from this mission of Jesús Carichíc to its* pueblos de visita *and* rancherías. *I cannot describe the routes accurately nor do I know how many leagues it is from this mission to Nonoava, San Borja, Coyáchic, Temeichic, Siso-guichic, Pamachic and Norogachic. These missions are near and in the vicinity of Carichíc. But to state properly, clearly and distinctly the distances, routes and directions from one place to another, one would have to have a tame bumblebee or honeybee and watch the paths it followed.*

FATHER JUAN YSIDRO FERNÁNDEZ DE ABEE, S.J.
written from Mission Jesús Carichíc, July 8, 1744

OVERWHELMING. That is perhaps the word that best describes the impact on one's senses on seeing the Sierra Tarahumara for the first time from a small airplane buzzing along at 12,000 feet. Valleys are 7,000 and 8,000 feet high. Peaks rise above them another 1,000 or 2,000 feet. Rivers and smaller streams run across mountain meadows and occasionally slice their way past cliffs and spires of volcanic tuff, carving V-shaped wedges into portions of the terrain and providing an example in miniature of the more dramatic barrancas cut thousands of feet deep by the Urique, Batopilas, and Verde rivers farther to the south.

Here and there, water and wind have done wonderful things. There are weirdly-shaped spires, some looking from the air like great clusters of sharp-pointed spikes and others looking distinctly phallic. Some of the higher peaks are flat on top, not unlike green mesas. But often beneath them, and sometimes on nearly all sides of them, are twisting, snakelike canyons with hopelessly precipitous sides. The walls may be only 300 or 400 feet, but for all practical purposes, they are impassable to man. From point A to point B might be a mere five or six miles when connected by a straight line drawn on a flat map, but for a human being walking from one place to the other the real distance can

I

*River to the Río Grande*

*Spires on the Río Conchos*

Tarahumara 3

be double, triple, or quadruple that. Much of this sierra country is up and down. In places it even hangs over a little bit.

The predominant color on the ground is the green of oaks and pines and junipers. Its various shades fade off into blues in the more remote distances. In the winter there are both blankets and patches of snow, with the higher peaks fully covered all winter long. In mid- to late summer, after the rainy season has begun, streams are filled to overflowing and mountain springs are gushing.

Where streams have dissected the rocky crust of the earth to expose cliffs and spires there are a few yellows, oranges, and reds. And much of the earth, beneath the cover of the evergreens, is a rich brown. Green and blue, however, overpower all the rest. The Sierra Madre is also the sierra *verde* and sierra *azul*.

The sky, like the sky elsewhere in northwestern Mexico and the southwestern United States, is a turquoise blue. Winter can bring an enormous and uniform spread of dark clouds. Summer is the season of clouds capable of shedding more than an inch of rain in an hour. From my field notes:

> *. . . The whole region is covered with massive cumulus clouds, pitch black, with lightning darting in and out among them. They are to be avoided. We climb to 11,450 feet, where the air temperature is 46°F.*
>
> *Once in awhile we can see the ground, but as often as not everything beneath us is a solid, billowy white. Occasional mushroom clouds explode to 30,000 feet or more above sea level, considerably above the altitude at which we are flying. The pilot lets the plane climb to 12,200 feet, just 300 feet short of its maximum ability.*
>
> *He carefully picks his course through the clouds. At times we skirt the fluffy edges of one of the giant mushrooms, and as I look up from my front seat window I can see this enormous mountain of white mist whirling silently and hypnotically over our heads. At other times he puts the plane into a mushroom, and we fly virtually blind in the zero-visibility fog for a few moments before emerging into the sunlight on the other side [August 1, 1978].*

Once on the ground in mountains above 6,000 feet, impressions do not change much. The land remains overwhelming. It runs on without end. The green and blue and peaks and valleys and canyons stretch to every horizon. Only now the close terrain is more familiar and thereby more manageable. To one who knows the mountains and high plateaus of northeastern Arizona and northwestern New Mexico, this is more like it. Somewhere in the distance someone is burning juniper or pinyon, and the unmistakable and pleasant aroma signals Navajoland, or the Pueblo Indian or Hispanic settlements of northern New Mexico, or, as it turns out, the sierra home of the Tarahumara.

As in most forests of the Southwest, there is little vegetation on the ground. The stands of timber are open. Only in the valleys and meadows, where there are no trees, is there a good cover of grasses and weeds. The forests themselves are chiefly of pine, richly furnished with such trees as Arizona, ponderosa, Engelmann, Lumholtz, Apache, Chihua-

Tarahumara

*Where the mesa meets the sky*

Tarahumara  5

hua, and pinyon pines, to say nothing of juniper, mahogany, and a dozen different kinds of oak trees, the latter growing at slightly lower elevations.

It is not surprising that these are "commercial" forests, among the most important in Mexico, nor that the principal industry is forestry. Sawmills, both large and small, dot the region. Lumbermen, moving north and south of the railroad, the *Ferrocarril Chihuahua al Pacífico*, which bisects Tarahumara country from northeast to southwest, have followed mining roads into the sierra and built their own roads where none existed before. Some of the smaller mills operate only for three or four years before the supply of commercial timber near them is exhausted. Then, like Arabs folding their tents, the operators dismantle the equipment, move it, and reassemble it in some still-unexploited part of the forest. Pines that are typically from a foot-and-a-half to three feet in diameter and fifty feet tall provide the raw resource.

To the south of this upland country, and beneath the range of pines and oaks, lies the far more famous canyon country of the Tarahumaras. The Urique, Batopilas, and Verde rivers have severed the landscape on the western side of the Continental Divide to form spectacular barrancas, canyons that are less steep-sided and farther apart from rim to rim than implied in the Spanish concept of *cañon*. They are usually compared with Arizona's Grand Canyon of the Colorado River, and justifiably so. They are wider and equally deep in places from rim to bottom. To the human onlooker they can be quite as breathtaking. As elsewhere in the Sierra Tarahumara, the hues are chiefly green and blue and brown, and there are few of the brilliant colors which hallmark the Grand Canyon. Neither are there the incredibly narrow passages hemmed in by towering, sheer-walled cliffs so characteristic of Arizona's great attraction.

Even so, to view these barrancas is to acquire a lasting impression. A Jesuit priest who first saw the canyon of the Río Urique in 1684 called it a "stupendous gorge," and half-way down on a narrow trail he climbed off his mule, "sweating and trembling all over from fright. For there opened on the left a chasm the bottom of which could not be seen, and on the right rose perpendicular walls of solid rock."

Where there are remnants of the old plateau surface that have survived in the canyon country there are still pines and a few oaks. But half-way down the canyons acacias and mimosas predominate, and on or near the bottoms are many kinds of cactuses, kapok trees, great stands of cane, and other plants characteristic of the warm lower elevations of western Chihuahua. The climate in the canyon depths is subtropical and humid, with mild, dry winters and hot, rainy summers, in sharp contrast to the cool, semiarid uplands to the north.

The Sierra Madre is appropriately massive, just as a Mother Mountain should be. She gives birth to life not only for her residents, but for untold thousands of other Mexicans in the foothills and plains below. Her crust is the ultimate source of agricultural alluvium; she is the immediate source of life-giving water. Her timber provides lumber for countless uses; her mantle covers deposits of gold, silver, copper, and other minerals which since the seventeenth century have been a challenge to the ingenuity of miners.

First, however, and probably last as well, she is the eternal and everlasting home and provider of those who would run fleet-footed over her surface, the Tarahumara.

# 6 *Tarahumara*

# CHAPTER TWO

The Indians live at great distances, separated from each other and scattered. They prefer to live in the ravines and canyons and in the cold, inhospitable mountains where they have their dwellings. Their native simplicity, barbarity, laziness and sloth incline them to this in preference to being reduced to living a rational, civilized human life.

The fact that the children are raised from their first and tender years in the canyons without the slightest control and do not live in the pueblos shows how hard it is later on to bring them to live in their reductions and lead a Christian life. From infancy they are brought up to be mountain vagabonds with no training in either morals or proper conduct. They are worse than beasts because the animals at least acknowledge their subjection to those who put them in cages and govern them.

. . . [T]he royal ministers should cooperate with the armed forces and give aid to the tireless laborers in the vineyard [i.e., the missionaries] by ordering repeated expeditions into the sierra. They should remove the Indians from their canyons and use armed force to make them live together in pueblos. They should burn their hovels and granaries in which they keep their corn. Eight or ten soldiers ought to be stationed at this mission until the Indians learn to love their pueblo. If they flee from the pueblo after being settled there the soldiers ought to hunt them down and bring them back. In this way the will of Our Catholic Kings will be done and some useful purpose will be served by the sweat poured out by the padre missionaries for the salvation of the wretched Indians' souls. The ultimate purpose for which we were cre-

*ated will be attained, i.e., to serve God in this life and to enjoy him in the next.*

FATHER JUAN YSIDRO FERNÁNDEZ DE ABEE, S.J.
written from Mission Jesús Carichíc, July 8, 1744

REDUCCION. Simply translated into English, the word means "reduction." However, to a missionary in seventeenth or eighteenth century New Spain a "reduction" was a legally defined institution, and not merely the act of reducing something. Shortly after the Jesuits arrived in Asunción in Paraguay in 1588 they proceeded to gather as many as 100,000 Indian charges into mission villages or mission pueblos which came to be known as *reducciones*. Here they could be supervised in new methods of agriculture, in stock raising, and in European crafts. Here, as well, they could be taught the basics of Christian doctrine and could be exposed to Spanish forms of social and political organization or, as the missionaries conceived of it, to "civilized life."

The idea was to bring Indians from out of the wilderness, to "reduce" them to pueblos where they could be kept segregated from ordinary Spaniards and other Europeans and where they would be under sole charge of the father missionary. It was the job of the missionary to Christianize the Indians, thereby to save their souls from eternal hell, as well as to bring them to vassalage of the Crown of Spain.

Bringing the Indians to the Holy Faith and to royal vassalage was not a haphazard enterprise on the part of the Spaniards in the New World. Royal orders, the Laws of the Indies, and other laws promulgated in various provinces came to prescribe a mission system that was intended in a ten-year period to bring the Indians from a state of paganism and "primitive wildness" to a state of full assimilation and citizenship within the Spanish realm. The program called for progress by stages, beginning with a simple mission for pagans; proceeding either to a reduction or to a conversion (where Indians were already living in concentrated settlements) in which the rudiments of Christianity were taught; advancing to a *doctrina*, intended for the teaching of those at least partially instructed in the Catholic faith; and concluding with a curacy, a parish church presided over by secular clergy rather than by missionary priests.

History has shown that ten years for such a program was more often overly optimistic than not. In fact, in many areas of New Spain the system in its entirety never succeeded in attaining the intended goals. The Sierra Tarahumara was one such region.

The Tarahumaras had no way of knowing it, but the year 1572 was one of portent for them. That is when missionaries of the Society of Jesus, the Jesuits, arrived in Mexico. Twenty-one years later some of them had gone northward and established themselves in Guadiana, a city we know today as Durango. By 1598 the Jesuits had established a mission among the Tepehuan Indians at a place 110 miles northwest of Guidiana, one they christened Santa Catalina. The northern and northwestward movement continued until at last, in 1607, Father Juan Fonte visited the valley of San Pablo de Balleza, another 115 miles northwest of Santa Catalina. This marked the southern boundary of Tarahumara country at that time. It was, moreover, the border between warring factions of Tarahumaras and Tepehuanes. Fonte met with more than 800 Tarahumara men and counseled peace between them and their southern neighbors. Four years later, in 1611, he returned to the valley in an effort to persuade both nearby and distant Tarahumaras to settle there permanently. The mission program, complete with the concept of reduction or mission pueblo, had begun.

The scenario for the ensuing decades is one familiar to anyone to knows something of the history of European and American westward expansion in the United States. The policies of Spain toward Indians in her northward movement into North America were notably different than the policies of England, France, and the United States, but the end results were often similar. It became Spain's policy to incorporate Indians into the body politic and into the bosom of Christianity rather than to exclude the tribes and to treat them as if they constituted sovereign nations. But even so, as missionaries, miners, soldiers, and Spanish settlers advanced, Indians became disenfranchised and retreated.

When first encountered in the early seventeenth century by the Jesuits, the Tarahumaras occupied a vast area of the Sierra Madre on both sides of the Río Papigochic north of the 28th parallel to a point well beyond the 29th parallel of north latitude. Today the 28th parallel marks their northernmost boundary and they have lost all but the headwaters of the Papigochic. Similarly, in the opening years of the 1600s their eastern boundary enclosed the fertile foothill and plains country which included the Río Balleza, the Río Conchos some thirty miles downstream from its junction with the Balleza, and all of the headwater streams of the Río San Pedro. Now the San Pedro and its headwaters are lost to them. So are the Balleza and more than fifty miles of the Conchos.

Not that all was loss. In their decades-long retreat from north and east, they moved a little south into lands that had once been the homeland of Northern Tepehuanes as well as a little west into former homelands of such groups as the Tubares, Temoris, Guazapares, Chinipas, and Warihios. Their relatively small gains here became the losses of others in the pushing and shoving inevitably occasioned by the Old World's conquest of the New World.

Why did the Tarahumaras ultimately retreat from the Spaniards, ever withdrawing into the fastness of mountains and barrancas? Why did they not instead welcome the missionaries and other Spaniards with open arms? It was, in the opinion of Father Fernández de Abee, because of "their natural inclination to idleness, drunkenness, and the other vices. . . . They are ungrateful, dull, and stupid in understanding speech. . . . They are also very cunning and alert in evil things. They are much inclined to robbery [and] dishonesty. They have no sense of personal honor nor of the honor of their daughters."

The Jesuits moved tirelessly and relentlessly northward along the plains and foothills of eastern Tarahumara country. Like a litany of saints, names appeared on maps to signal the eventual loss of these places to their native inhabitants: San Miguel de Las Bocas and nearby San Gabriel (1630); San Felipe de Conchos, San Gerónimo de Huejotitlán, and San Pablo de Balleza (1639); San Javier Satevó (1640). Mines were discovered at Parral in 1631, and with the discovery came another gold rush like that to nearby Santa Bárbara in 1567. By 1638 the Tarahumaras were working as laborers in the Parral mines and digging canals around Parral and in the surrounding valleys. Other Tarahumaras entered into commerce with the Spanish miners, trading corn for wool, finished articles of clothing, and other goods.

*Shepherds watch their flock*

10   *Tarahumara*

*Francisco Torres Batista*

In 1645 one Jesuit complained that some Tarahumaras had been forced to work for two months without pay in the Parral mines and had been told they would have to work another two months or not be paid at all. And in 1649, five Tarahumaras, who may have been captured as rebellious Indians, were apparently owned as slaves by a Parral miner.

The greatest effect of Parral on the Tarahumaras, however, lay not so much in the direct contact they had with the mining city as in the influx of Spaniards it brought to the region generally. This influx included more Jesuit missionaries, and Parral became the springboard from which Christian doctrine and Spanish culture jumped into the Sierra Tarahumara.

The "ungrateful, dull, and cunning" Tarahumara, some of whom had been conscripted as laborers, others of whom had known the status of slave, and still others who had survived a great epidemic of 1638 when Spanish-introduced disease raged among their settlements, did not take matters passively. In 1648 Tarahumaras staged the first of many revolts, attacking initially at a place southwest of Parral before sweeping the countryside almost as far north as the Río Conchos. This revolt brought the Spaniards into the heart of the Sierra Tarahumara, and a Spanish general made his headquarters at Carichíc, high in the mountains near the headwaters of the Río San Ignacio, itself a northern tributary of the Conchos.

In 1649 the Governor of Nueva Vizcaya, the province of New Spain which included the Sierra Tarahumara, raided with his troops as far north and west as the Río Papigochic on the western side of the Continental Divide. His soldiers, both Spanish and Indian, killed ten Tarahumaras, took twenty-seven of them prisoner, and rampaged over the countryside, wasting it. They demanded, and received, the heads of two of four known rebel leaders. The mountain stronghold had been breached, never again to be free of foreigners. And the breach was a most violent one.

During the thirty-six years after 1648 the Jesuits added more placenames to their growing list of what were presumed to be spiritual conquests: San Bernabé, Cusihuiriachic, Coyáchic, Temóchic, Santo Tomás, Papigochic, Mátachic, Carichíc, Norogachic, Nonoava, Bocoyna, and Sisoguichic, to list only a few. And along the way there were martyred priests and martyred Tarahumara leaders and followers. In 1652 there was a major uprising in the Tarahumara northwest led by a man named Tepóraca. Spanish soldiers eventually inflicted heavy losses on the natives, and when the latter sued for peace, it was granted only on the condition that they bring Tepóraca as a prisoner to the Spaniards. They agreed, and in a few days the rebel chieftain was handed over. He was sentenced to hang, and with the rope around his neck his captives exhorted him—as a one-time Christian—to repent his sins that his soul might not go to hell. According to historian Peter Dunne, ". . . his heart was of flint and he would not yield. He was hanged, therefore, to the limb of a tree, cursing the Spaniards as long as he had breath to draw and damning the cowardice of his tribesmen for making peace with the invader. He died hating his own for their treachery and betrayal of himself." Having died unrepentant, his soul therefore most surely destined for an eternity of damnation, his suspended corpse was riddled with arrows and allowed to hang until it rotted away.

In 1684 and 1687 two more nails were driven into what was becoming the northern

Tarahumara coffin. In the first of these years there was a silver strike at San Ignacio Coyáchic; in 1687 there was a second rush for mineral riches to San Bernabé Cusihuiria-chic. Miners poured into the country without regard for Tarahumaras and any rights they might have. Indeed, just as they had been needed at Parral, so were they needed here to mine, to strip the countryside of timbers needed for the mines, and to labor in making bricks. They were pressed into unwilling service as domestics while both miners and Spanish ranchers preempted their best farmlands. The Spanish merchants who followed close on the heels of the miners did their part to draw Tarahumaras further into the web of Spanish economy and dependence.

Once again, this time in 1690, the natives rebelled. Two priests were killed and the bloodshed on both sides—not to mention the atrocities—was horrible. An uneasy peace prevailed for seven years until 1697 when the Tarahumaras along the Río Papigochic "broke out" once more. Battles raged both here and in and near Sisoguichic. In March of 1697 the Spaniard in command in the Papigochic area tried to bring matters to a halt by shooting thirty Indians, cutting off their heads, and impaling them on spears in one of the settlements and along one of the more-traveled roads. Although intended as an object lesson, it had quite the opposite effect. The rebellion continued and in June, 1698, the Tarahumaras pillaged the mission pueblo of Sisoguichic. It was not until later that year that the fighting ceased. Its cessation proved to be the last major military effort on the part of the Tarahumaras to rid themselves of Spanish control. Their modes of defense instead became passive resistance, withdrawal and avoidance.

In 1709 silver was discovered at the site of modern Chihuahua City, and there were still more demands on Tarahumaras for their labor. Many of them, both here and in the southeast, gave up the cultural ghost and disappeared into the lower socioeconomic class of the general population of Mexico. How many Tarahumaras voluntarily relinquished their cultural identity, through intermarriage or otherwise, no one will ever know. Certainly many of them did so. But just as certainly, many more had "hearts of flint and would not yield."

Even the cultural conservatives, however, remained indelibly stamped by the immediate effects of a hundred years of Spanish presence. In 1611 Father Fonte reported that Tarahumara women were excellent weavers, but the material from which they wove was agave fiber. By 1625 a few of them were weaving wool into clothing and blankets. Tara-humaras were raising Spanish fowl and sheep. Aboriginal farming methods, depending on the particular locality, probably consisted of flood plain farming and dry farming. The latter was carried out in rock-walled terraces or in fields where trees had been felled and burned. By 1638 many Tarahumaras had been exposed to irrigation agriculture, with men employed in the construction of canals. New building techniques using bricks and adobe were also introduced early in the seventeenth century. By the middle of that same century sheep, oxen, cows, horses, burros, and mules had been brought into the Sierra Tarahumara by Spanish rancher-settlers. Tarahumaras were quick to appropriate these animals, especially the sheep, for their own.

No later than the early 1700s, Tarahumaras in some areas had added wheat to the inventory of their basic native crops of corn, beans, and squash, even as they had added hide drums, violins, and harps to their list of musical instruments. Also early in the eighteenth century, possibly after 1725, large numbers of goats were brought into Tarahumara country and simultaneously the numbers of sheep increased.

Just as Spaniards introduced oxen, so did they bring in the plow, yoke, and harness needed to plow with oxen. Peaches, apples, oranges, quinces, pears, lemons, limes, watermelons, potatoes, new varieties of beans, and even weeds from the Old World were added to the native diet in the seventeenth and eighteenth centuries. Spanish religious rituals and beliefs and elements of Spanish political structure became selectively integrated into Tarahumara culture. Some community leaders accepted the alien title of "governor" and canes became a symbol of authority in office. Among "Christian" Tarahumaras, Holy Week and the feasts of Guadalupe, Christmas, and Epiphany became important times in the ceremonial calendar.

Finally, the Spaniards introduced iron tools such as knives and hoes, the axe preeminent among them. The axe enabled people to fell trees with comparative ease and to work them into shapes suitable for the construction of storage facilities, houses, plows, bowls, musical instruments, and other wooden implements.

These were the "blessings" of Spanish culture that Tarahumaras selectively adopted and adapted. Less than blessings were epidemics which swept the region, five in the seventeenth century alone, and the conscription of labor. The latter was viewed with a jaundiced eye by the natives and vocally opposed by the missionaries. Father Fernández de Abee complained of the situation in 1744:

> . . . [The Tarahumaras] always avoid being recruited on orders the Governor [of Nueva Viscaya] is always giving. He calls for 50 or 20 Indians and the alcalde mayor [mayor] of the mining town of Cusiguriachic wants ten. All this is contrary to the Laws of the Indies and the Royal Cédulas which insist that no more than four percent of the Indians be taken from the [mission] pueblos. But the orders force them to leave to labor in the mines or the coal pits. Since they are forced to this by fear, in a few days they run away and hide in the thorny ravines to avoid being forced to return. There they are hidden for whole months without hearing mass or learning Christian doctrine. . . . Just when they are learning to like the pueblo and are learning all the things taught by the padre minister, there comes an order or warrant from the Governor of the realm. At the same time another order comes from the alcalde mayor of the mining town of Cusiguriachic for 60 Indians to be sent to one place and 30 to another. Thus, in a single instant all that was accomplished with extreme effort is destroyed.

In 1767 King Charles III of Spain, for a variety of reasons, some of them known to him alone, issued an order calling for the removal of the Jesuits from all of New Spain. In the Tarahumara country this meant that some of the mission stations were elevated to the status of parishes or curacies and handed over to the secular clergy. Others, however, were turned over to Franciscan missionaries to carry on the work begun more than 150 years earlier by the Society of Jesus. By 1777 Franciscans were working in at least fourteen Tarahumara missions, Tutuaca, Tónachic, Batopilillas, Baqueachic, Cerocahui, and Nabogame among them. Their efforts, however, were comparatively short-lived. They were a part of New Spain, and the days of New Spain herself were numbered. Mexico's revolution for independence began in 1810; it came to a successful Mexican conclusion in 1821. Given the remoteness of the Sierra Tarahumara from Mexico's population centers, it is not surprising that little seems to have been written about the region during these troublous times. What is clear is that the Franciscans, too, relinquished the missions.

With the missionaries gone, the Chihuahuan government, on paper at least, turned to Mexican settlers to bring about "instruction and civilization of the Indians." This was one of the stated purposes of the 1825 Law of Colonization intended to bring about the economic development of the state by offering settlers lands in more remote areas. Indians could also be given title to lands, but few of them were. "The net effect of the Law of Colonization," writes anthropologist Edward Spicer, "was to encourage Mexicans to move deeper into Tarahumara country, to push the Indians farther west and south into the mountains, and to intensify the old settler-Indian conflict. . . . From this point on through the 1800's the process of voluntary isolation from Mexicans on the part of the great majority of Tarahumaras was intensified. Some Indians left the rancherías and became absorbed in the population of the Mexican towns, but the majority withdrew to the extent that they could."

Toward the end of the nineteenth century both church and state began to take a renewed interest in the Tarahumaras. In 1899 the governor of Chihuahua saw to the establishment of a school at Tónachic; in 1903 two schools followed elsewhere. The Jesuits, having returned to Mexico in the nineteenth century, reentered the Sierra Tarahumara in 1900. They reopened missions, established an orphanage, built schools, and started hospitals and clinics, all activities which continue today. Governor Enrique C. Creel established a new settlement in Tarahumara country as a "colony" ideally composed of 75 percent Tarahumaras and 25 percent Mexicans, each family to have ten hectares of land. But a year later, in 1907, Creel—the name of the new settlement—had 191 people divided into 30 Tarahumara and 21 Mexican families. The proportions were destined to change dramatically to favor the Mexicans. Modern Creel is best characterized as an important Mexican lumber and railroad town in the Sierra Madre.

The wake of the 1910 Mexican revolution brought with it some land reform that made its way to the Tarahumaras. The Mexican *ejido*, or communal land, system was imposed upon them, and they were thereby given a way to legalize their titles both to land and to livestock. They were also given a new political figure in the form of the communal land commissioner *(el comisariado ejidal)*, a native person whose major job it would be to mediate between fellow Tarahumaras and the outside world—especially in matters concerning land and its use.

Since 1910 there have been efforts to bring together disparate and distant segments of the Tarahumara population into a single political or psychological entity. To this end there have been congresses of Tarahumara people, the seventh one having been held as recently as 1972.

*Tarahumara* 15

But the most startling fact concerning the events of Tarahumara history is that they have fostered cultural stability rather than change. It is likely that if the Father Fonte of 1607 were to visit many Tarahumara communities of today he would find more that seemed familiar than otherwise. And could Father Fernández de Abee of 1744 survey the Sierra Tarahumara scene in 1978, he would still complain of those recalcitrant Indians who "live at great distances, separated from each other and scattered," and who still "prefer to live in the ravines and canyons and in the cold, inhospitable mountains where they have their dwellings."

Tarahumara

# CHAPTER THREE

*I*ndians, Indians, the goddamned Indians. As if we don't have enough to worry about without them on our hands, and hearts and minds, as well. The one thing we could do for these people, I am thinking as I trudge along at the rear of the column, the one and only decent thing we could do for them (and by "we" I mean mainly the Mexicans and Mexican "authorities," but to include gringo Americans and Europeans, too), is to leave them alone. Throw out the teachers, the missionaries, the government doctors and public health technicians, close off the roads and stop the road-building, stop the logging, shut down the mines, burn down the hotels, tear up the airstrips, throw out the totalitarian fanatics from so-called "third world" politics, ban all tourists, including us, and leave these people alone. Leave them alone.

But leaving them alone, that is the one thing we will not do. So the Indians are doomed. The Tarahumara, unless saved by a quick collapse of the world industrial mega-machine now moving in on them, haven't a fucking chance. Like the Guarani-Tupi of the Amazon, like the Kurds of Iran or Iraq, like the herdsmen of Tibet, like the Hopi of Arizona, like a hundred other small and once-independent tribes around the globe, these Indians are going to be . . . incorporated.

DOOMSAYERS HAVE BEEN WRITING the Tarahumaras off, or predicting their imminent demise, since the nineteenth century. "Since one of the richest mining districts of the world lies near the land I have briefly described," wrote explorer Frederick Schwatka in

1892, "it will not be long before the age of steam and electricity will replace the age of stone." Naturalist Carl Lumholtz gave them only a century after the 1890s before all the Tarahumaras would "be made the servants of the whites and disappear."

Beginning in the 1870s a great mining boom began in the Sierra Tarahumara. Concessions offered by Mexican president Porfirio Díaz attracted foreign capital and foreign industrial know-how to the barrancas and mountains to plumb them for gold, silver, and other metals and minerals. These mines became the magnet that attracted thousands of Mexicans to Tarahumara country and islands of Mexican culture were scattered everywhere in what had been a veritable fastness. Mexicans worked in the mines; other Mexicans became involved in ranching, farming, and commerce to supply the mining towns. The Indians either withdrew or were forced to withdraw. By the 1890s the Mexicans had appropriated the best farming and pasture lands for themselves.

Left with no other alternative, Tarahumaras in substantial numbers began to sell their labor for products or cash. They worked in the mines as laborers or as field hands or servants on Mexican ranches and farms. They learned Spanish, began to wear Mexican clothing, and took their first major steps on the road to assimilation. Some of them, in fact, went all the way, and their descendants today are Mexicans rather than Indians.

But the world economy and society upon which successful mining depends are fickle things. By 1914 the price of silver had fallen; Mexico was suffering through the wake of a revolution which had seen the departure of Porfirio Díaz. Mining all but collapsed. The Mexicans either went away or became small farmers or merchants in the sierra. The small farmers either bought parcels of land from Mexicans with large landholdings or they moved in on Mexican ranches as sharecroppers, thus avoiding further conflict with the Tarahumaras.

When Bennett and Zingg arrived in the Sierra Tarahumara in 1930 they marvelled that so many Tarahumaras continued to live the kind of life described for them by Lumholtz in the 1890s. And it was in the 1930s that playwright Antonin Artaud wrote, "This race [Tarahumara], which ought to be physically degenerate, has for four hundred years resisted every force that has come to attack it: civilization, interbreeding, war, winter, animals, storms, and the forest."

After World War II, "development" began again. Not only was mining reactivated, but the trees of the mountains came to be labeled "timber." Mexico pushed into the area from the east with roads, railroads, and airstrips. In 1961 the last link was formed in the *Ferrocarril Chihuahua al Pacífico*, a 565-mile-long railroad tying Ojinago, Chihuahua, and its neighboring city of Presidio, Texas, to Topolobampo, Sinaloa, on the west coast of Mexico. It runs diagonally through the heart of Tarahumara country, going from southwest to northeast. Highways are not far behind, and it won't be many years after 1978 before it will be as easy to drive into the Sierra Tarahumara from the Sonoran side on the west as it is already to drive in from the east.

One observer has written that in recent years the problems of the Tarahumaras have been aggravated "by erosion caused by wasteful agricultural technology and the careless stripping of timber of Mexican lumber companies that began operations in some parts of the Sierra in the early 1940s."

18   *Tarahumara*

The train and the improvement of roads have brought with them an influx of tourists, although they rarely get beyond where the roads and train can take them. In 1978 a Los Angeles, California, entrepreneur brought in two busloads of California tourists to a Tarahumara community to watch the Holy Week celebration. Some of the tourists were under the impression the Indians were staging a pageant for their benefit. They barged in, cameras blazing. The Tarahumaras retaliated in part by charging each tourist $25.00 pesos (about $1.00) to be there.

The lack of sanitation in the region provides at least some check on tourism. Parasites, diarrhea, dysentary, and typhoid fever are always possibilities.

Both Mexican federal schools and health care facilities and Jesuit schools, health care facilities, and missions are ever-present forces in the Sierra Tarahumara working to promote change that is defined by them as "progressive." There are others, including Tarahumaras themselves, who are slowly working toward some kind of political structure that will include all Tarahumaras, something in the form of a Tarahumara congress. As well-meaning as all of these attempts doubtless are, experience among Indians in the United States shows that such attempts often have unanticipated and undesirable consequences. Many tribal governments in the United States exist to the detriment of local community governments. Although most Tarahumaras, from the official Mexican point of view, live in ejidos, some of which even own sawmills as a cooperative enterprise, one of the major factors in their cultural survival has been the looseness and flexibility of their social and political system. They have no clans or lineages and they reckon descent and inheritance on both sides of the family. From the family-household to the ranch or pueblo to the network of people who customarily drink corn beer together—these are the affective outline of Tarahumara social and political life. Such a community of people, whose economy depends largely on subsistence and barter, demands face-to-face cooperation. So does it allow for the maximum dignity and self-respect of the individual.

Most of the conscious purveyors of change among the Tarahumaras mean only well. This was true for the seventeenth-century Jesuits who were concerned for Tarahumaras' souls as it is for today's dedicated teacher in a Tarahumara school. However, as historian Robert Archibald has noted, "The principle emerges that decent peoples whose motives as judged by their own standards are excellent, have frequently violated other people who live by different standards."

Anthropologist John Kennedy is nearly as sanguine as Edward Abbey about the prospects for the Tarahumara future:

> The Indians in the recent past achieved a modicum of equilibrium with their environment, with reasonable adjustments to the gradual increase of mestizos in their country. This balance is now being upset. The familiar pattern of the Third World is being reenacted once again in the sierra, and with the same disastrous results. Lumber and commercial interests have replaced the mining of the early period as the economic incentives for exploitation of the Indians and their native resources. These interests are accompanied by the inevitable influx of tourists into this wild, beautiful land.

*All of these scourges are sometimes reinforced in many of their effects by the well-intentioned programs of the government and the church. The introduction of modern medicine and education is changing the Indians' population balance, transforming the system of wants, and producing another exploitable class with no skills to sell at the bottom of the social ladder in northwest Mexico. The spread of commercial alcohol is disastrous in conjunction with native drinking patterns, and the shy and politically helpless Tarahumara have little recourse against the aggressive incursion of more powerful elements into their once isolated country.*

As our small plane was making its way back from one of our trips into the Sierra Tarahumara, I found myself deeply troubled. Is what we are doing, I wondered, including presenting these gentle and hospitable people to a wider world through the photographs and words of a book, the right thing to do? I come to at least one decision and record it in my field book:

*We are going to conceal the placenames of the ranchos and pueblos we have visited. Partly, it is to offer these selfless and innocent people some measure of protection against a possible onslaught of exploiters and curiosity seekers our book may inspire. But in a broader sense, it is because placenames are irrelevant. Tarahumara is not merely a place; it is a state of mind and being. Whether one glimpses the depths of the Urique Canyon or the Place of the Wild Onions is not so important as knowing there are still places in the world where people are their unfettered selves.*

*"Simplify, simplify, simplify," we are admonished by Thoreau. The Tarahumaras are the personification of his advice. Their lives are an uncluttered example for all of us, whether they live in the Place of the Nut Tree or the Place of the Pinnacles, and whether we live in Tucson, Arizona, or Buffalo, New York.*

People who use caves for shelter and oxen to plow and who grow their own corn, squash, and beans seem wonderfully exotic to us. But after spending some time with them and returning to what we are wont to call "civilization," one realizes that it is we who are exotic and not they. Everything Tarahumaras do makes simple and direct sense. One need not be an anthropologist nor a psychologist to perceive the relationships between their activities and their physical and social environment. We, on the other hand, are given to doing many things for reasons none of us can really understand. Large numbers of us live long lives of what Thoreau called "quiet desperation," or even long lives of noisy desperation. Tarahumaras' lives may be shorter, but they are not desperate.

Ironically, most of the changes one can see taking place in the lives of modern Tarahumaras are not those resulting from conscious attempts of people to change them. They

20   *Tarahumara*

are instead being fostered by the Tarahumaras' own adjustments to new economic realities and by their own desires to have for themselves many things they are unable to produce. Coca-Cola can stand as the symbol for Faro cigarettes, chewing gum, canned lard, canned sardines, canned chilis, noodles, wheat flour, portable radios and batteries, coffee, aspirin, potato chips, and Alka Seltzer. And who are we to say these people should not be able to buy crucifixes and statues of saints, soap, manta cloth, needles, thread, yarn, dyes, blankets, dried meat, mirrors, and Mexican clothes? Indeed, who really has the right to judge they would be better off staying away from schools, churches, hospitals, and clinics?

Tarahumaras may well be in a unique position among the indigenous populations of the Americas. Potentially they have options open to them closed to other peoples. They may be able to choose individually whether they wish to remain secure in their mountain home, farming and drinking corn beer as they have always done, or to migrate to sawmill, Mexican ranch or city to become assimilated into the mainstream of Mexican national life. Between these "either-or" extremes lie many additional possibilities.

Nearly every adult Tarahumara is a craftsperson. They weave woolen blankets, although no rugs, of high quality. Their pottery, presently more functional than decorative, is firm and sturdy. With encouragement, some of their production could become an art form in the non-Indian market. Their baskets are lovely and utilitarian. The women are folk artists *par excellence* with needle and embroidery thread. Their woven sashes and sewn blouses might in some circles be considered *haute couture*. Wood carvers have demonstrated their ingenuity by shaping whimsical little figures out of pine bark to sell to tourists who arrive in Creel or Divisadero.

There may be a market in the offing for such products well beyond the isolated confines of the Sierra Tarahumara. For many years traders and other middlemen have dealt with Tarahumaras for their arts and crafts, but only on the most limited basis. Today there is talk of the formation of craft cooperatives in some communities and ways are being sought to reduce the profits of entrepreneurs greatly while encouraging the production of crafts the average consumer could afford to buy.

Should any of this come about, and the beginnings are already seen, Tarahumaras could derive sufficient cash income to take up the slack in their barter and subsistence economy. It would be possible for people who choose to do so to remain in place while selling the products of one's highly skilled craft, all the while continuing a life-style whose benefits have been demonstrated for more than 300 years. Mahatma Gandhi called such efforts "cottage industries." The experiment seems to have failed for a teeming India, but cottage industries might well succeed in the Sierra Tarahumara. For those individuals who prefer to trade sandals for shoes and disappear into the Mexican night, the choice would remain open. But for the stubborn ones, so might there be a way.

# CHAPTER FOUR

*The Tarahumare in his native condition is many times better off, morally, mentally, and economically, than his civilised brother; but the white man will not let him alone as long as he has anything worth taking away. Only those who by dear experience have learned to be cautious are able to maintain themselves independently; but such cases are becoming more and more rare.*

*It is the same old story over again, in America, as in Africa and Asia, and everywhere. The simple-minded native is made the victim of the progressive white, who, by fair means or foul, deprives him of his country. Luckily, withal, the Tarahumare has not yet been wiped out of existence. His blood is fused into the working classes of Mexico, and he grows a Mexican. But it may take a century yet before they will all be made the servants of whites and disappear. . . . Their assimilation may benefit Mexico, but one may well ask: Is it just? Must the weaker always be first crushed, before he can be assimilated by the new condition of things?*

CARL SOPHUS LUMHOLTZ
*Unknown Mexico, 1902*

CARL LUMHOLTZ, Norwegian naturalist and explorer, spent most of the first three years of the 1890s among the Tarahumaras. His ruminations concerning their ultimate fate are as apropos now as they were then. Perhaps more so. Nearly a hundred years have gone by since he tramped the mountains and barrancas of the Sierra Tarahumara, and these remarkable people whom he came to know and to respect have not been wiped out of existence, nor are they all the servants of whites. But the questions Lumholtz posed about the presumed need of the "progressive" white to deprive Tarahumaras of their country, of their dignity and self-respect, and even of their very identity remain unanswered.

He was not the first English-speaking scientific observer to take an interest in these people. In 1885 a physician-turned botanist named Edward Palmer made collections of plants in the Sierra Madre Occidental. Judging from Palmer's well-known interest in Indians of the American Southwest, it is virtually certain that Palmer paid attention to the Tarahumaras, especially their use of plants, although he left us no published record of these efforts.

Palmer was followed in 1890 by another physician and former soldier, this one turned adventurer and journalist, named Frederick Schwatka. Schwatka made a long circuit by mule back through the mountains and down into the barrancas, and he reported his trip in a popular book called *In the Land of Cave and Cliff Dwellers.* He showed himself to be the consummate tourist. He marvelled at the scenery, talked with Mexicans and Americans—the latter then running the mines at Batopilas, and caught but fleeting glimpses of the Tarahumaras except for those who were "civilized," Indians who had integrated themselves into the Mexican mining economy or who otherwise associated permanently with Mexican towns and ranches. The "savage" Tarahumaras, as he called the others, seem largely to have eluded him.

Notwithstanding the tourist nature of Schwatka's journey, he persuaded a small group of Tarahumaras living near Yoquivo above the barranca of the Río Batopilas to go with him to be "exhibited" in Chicago as "representative cave-dwellers." Two years later Lumholtz met one of the men who had been to Chicago, and he asked him about his experience. What impressed the Tarahumara most was the "big water," Lake Michigan, near which those people dwelled. He had enjoyed riding on trains but complained that he had not been fed enough. "His experience on the trip," wrote Lumholtz, "had familiarised him with the white man and his queer, incomprehensible ways, and made him something of a philosopher."

It was Carl Lumholtz, Schwatka's immediate successor, who brought the Tarahumara to the attention of a truly wide reading audience. He wrote four articles about his travels in the Sierra Tarahumara for the popular *Scribner's Magazine*, and his two-volume work, *Unknown Mexico*, first published in 1902, captured worldwide interest and acquainted thousands of readers with "the American cave-dwellers." Both volumes were published in a Norwegian language edition in 1903; a London edition in English appeared at the same time. The following year it came out in Spanish. The English version, with the addition of maps, prefatory material, and eighteen color plates, was reprinted in 1973 by the Rio Grande Press of New Mexico.

Since the days of Lumholtz there have been three major works in English concerning the Tarahumara, two of them by anthropologists and one by a geographer. The first is the anthropological study by Wendell C. Bennett and Robert M. Zingg, *The Tarahumara* (1935); the second is *The Tarahumar of Mexico*, by geographer Campbell W. Pennington (1963); and the third is anthropologist John G. Kennedy's *Tarahumara of the Sierra Madre* (1978). When viewed together, these books portray an extraordinary span of cultural continuity and stability over the past ninety years. Although it was doubtless

a journalistic exaggeration on the parts of Schwatka and Lumholtz to characterize Tarahumaras as "cave dwellers," the fact remains that some Tarahumaras did use caves as
dwelling sites. They still do. But their use of caves or, more correctly, rock shelters, is
merely one small example of a much greater truth concerning these people. It is that they
are complete pragmatists, and it is this pragmatism in their relationships to one another
and to their environment that has allowed them to live so well for so long in their Chihuahuan mountain fastness. Had only Father Fernández de Abee and the other seven-
teenth- and eighteenth-century Jesuits understood this guiding principle of Tarahumara

life they would have wondered less at the failure of reducción. The Tarahumaras knew
from long experience what the missionaries were never forced to learn, i.e., a scattered
existence—with its many social consequences—is the only kind guaranteed to permit
survival in the Sierra Tarahumara without the need for continued outside subsidies. Subsistence farmers, such as the Tarahumaras were and continue to be, cannot afford the lux-
ury of urban living.

Modern Tarahumara settlements are referred to either as *pueblos* or *ranchos*. All
pueblos have a church; all of them have a *comunidad*, a place where people convene to
discuss matters of concern to residents of the pueblo or of ranchos who perceive the pueblo as their governmental center. The comunidad may take the form of a courthouse,
jail building, a wing attached to a church structure, or some open-air site where people
may gather conveniently. Pueblos vary considerably in size as well as in the degree to
which their populations are concentrated. Those with resident missionaries or government agents and such additional facilities as schools, hospitals, or clinics have greater
population densities. Where there are large numbers of Mexicans or mestizoized Tara-

humaras, the natives still involved in more traditional subsistence and barter economy live on the fringes of town in separate ranchos.

Ranchos are simply residence groups loosely clustered at a site where there is sufficient land to farm. As with the pueblo, the basic unit of society in a rancho is the household made up of a nuclear family, usually a mother, father, their children, and perhaps one or both of the parents of either spouse. Most households typically have about five people living in them; ranchos may have as few as two or three households or as many as fifteen or twenty. Pueblos, generally situated where there are more arable lands, are likely to have at least a dozen households.

In the real world, the division of Tarahumara settlements into pueblos and ranchos of the kinds described here may be too simple. In their own language, the people speak simply of a *betechi* or *beterachi*, from *bete*, ''to reside,'' *chi* or *rachi*, ''place of.'' A betechi is a ranch, farm, or small farm, simply because that is where most Tarahumaras live. But ''home place'' might be a better translation.

Each such place has a name. Moreover, a named place may consist of a single household. By way of example, within less than a mile of one another are four ''ranchos'' with different names: Place of the Walnut Tree, Wild Onion, Place of the Spires, and Place of the Caves. The first consists of two households and the latter of one household each, the last actually being a cave dwelling. The people in all five households are related either by blood or marriage. Their ceremonial and governmental affiliation is with a ''pueblo'' a few miles downstream, a place where there is a church and school.

The Sierra Tarahumara is covered by 15 of Chihuahua's 67 *municipios*, a municipio being analogous to a county in the United States. There are at least 2,000 ranchos in these 15 municipios, with the number being much higher were one to include every Tarahumara named homestead. Looking down on the mountains from the air in a small plane, two impressions stand out above all others. The first is the massiveness and vastness of the Sierra Madre itself; the second are these hundreds of widely scattered houses and fences and fields, nearly all of them at isolating distances from one another and yet connected by an incredible network of trails, most of them nothing more than footpaths. There are literally thousands of miles of such trails in the mountains and barrancas. They are the threads in the web of Tarahumara settlement.

It is typical to see from one to three or four small log cabins or stone or adobe houses within a mile of one another, each standing in its own yard enclosed by a fence of brush, rocks, or wooden poles. Near each house in the mountain uplands stands at least one granary which is built of hand-hewn wooden planks or, more rarely, of rocks and mud. A wooden chicken coop elevated off the ground, a wooden platform in which freshly harvested corn is laid to dry before it is stored in the granary, and a simple corral of poles in which livestock—chiefly goats and sheep—are kept for the night, are common.

Near these households are agricultural fields. Some are at dizzying elevations on the flat tops of mountains; others cling stubbornly to mountain slopes where hand-built terraces mark their contours; and still others are snuggled along the edges of streams in the mountain valleys. No highways carry the crops to market; no roads take the farmer to his field. The farmer is his own market and a Rarámuri, a foot runner of seemingly end-

26   *Tarahumara*

less energy, needs only a trail to accommodate his oxen and his rubber tire-soled sandals.

In the few places where a road or a railroad exist there are mines or lumber towns or centers of Jesuit or Mexican governmental activity. Their bearing stands in sharp, concentrated contrast to the Tarahumara presence. Mexicans live on the land; Tarahumaras live off of it. A Mexican community in these mountains is a geographical reality. A Tarahumara community, in opposition to geography, is better defined in terms of people who interact in ways that are uniquely their own.

To understand other people it is necessary to get out of an airplane or to climb down from a mule, burro, or horse and to meet them on their own terms. In the case of the Tarahumara, this means on foot. Such an encounter, accompanied by a willingness to share the people's own life-style, will engender mutual understanding.

The hike down the canyon from the summit trailhead was not really a long one. It only seemed that way at first because we were tramping off into the unknown with no map and no immediate guide. Directions and descriptions had been pointed out from the mountain top where we stood with a friend who had been there before. Our vantage point, marked by a large wooden cross, overlooked other mountains, canyons, mesas, and a river valley. It was where one bids God for a safe journey or gives thanks for a safe return after a steep climb up the slope below.

Once down the slope, there was a stream in a narrow canyon. To become lost was impossible. This was the only stream, and it was our conduit. There were trails on either bank, but they all led the same way and to the same places. We walked happily along, the whole world to ourselves except for birds, the spectacular coppery-tailed trogon among them. Here and there the stream had to be forded and there were pauses to drink its fresh, cold water. Its miniature waterfalls were a joy to behold.

The trees, shrubs, and wildflowers on both sides of the stream were beautiful, including lavender-barked madrones and many kinds of oaks as well as pinyons and junipers. These were below the predominantly pine-studded region at the trailhead. Cool rocks were covered with lichens. Many kinds of mosses and ferns, including horsetail ferns, grew at the water's edge.

It was August, and as elsewhere in what North Americans call the "Greater Southwest," it was the rainy season. If as many as twenty inches of rain were to fall here each year, probably the case in this particular spot, a fourth of that could be expected to fall in July, a fourth in August, and the remaining ten inches pretty evenly distributed throughout the other ten months. But as Tarahumara corn farmers know, what can be expected to happen on the average over a normal lifespan does not necessarily happen every year. If the right amount of rain could be relied upon to fall at the right time each year, that farmer's normal lifespan might be lengthened beyond its present forty-five years.

This had been one of the "not normal" years. There was plenty of rain in late July. Almost too much. But there hadn't been a proper downpour in May and June to insure a really healthy growth of corn planted in March or April. The stalks were up during our visit, but they were stunted and their ears were few. Some were already yellowing, more likely to end up as animal fodder than as corn for human consumption.

*Tarahumara*  27

*Collapsing church and an abandoned school in a Tarahumara pueblo*

28   Tarahumara

For one or two miles, except for the trail itself there was no sign of human activity, past or present. At a place where the canyon eventually widened were the remains of a fence made of wooden poles. This fence enclosed a tiny field. Rocks along the edge of the field just above the stream suggested this had once been a small terrace. The rocks, carefully placed by human hands, had trapped soil washing off the canyon slope and had, for a while, been able to nourish a few crops of corn, beans, or squash. If so, it had been a garden, really, rather than a "field."

Or the enclosed area may simply have been a corral. Our amateur archaeological efforts proved inconclusive.

In another half mile there was more evidence of man: a small rock shelter that had once been used for some kind of storage; a pine log notched into a ladder; and a pair of domesticated burros. Sitting for a moment to escape the increasing heat, we noticed a strange rock, a veritable stone artifact, circular and about five inches in diameter, flat on one of its surfaces and convex on the other. It had been shaped by using another rock to strike flakes from its edges. It became a mystery to be solved.

A half mile more and about four lazy backpacking hours from the wooden cross at the trailhead, the stream came around a bend and slowed its downhill rush where the canyon broadened into a narrow valley. On the downstream right bank the ground was level enough to support several acres of bean plants and, below that, many more acres of corn. Both plants and stalks were green; the beans hugged the ground while the stalks were about four feet high. Upslope from the fields, toward the rocks and scattered pine trees, there were two figures clothed in skirts and blouses tending a mixed flock of black, white, and tan goats and sheep. With the help of a couple of nondescript dogs these two barefooted girls, sisters, kept the thirty or so animals in the flock moving to where they could eat only grass, flowers, and weeds, not letting them pause long enough in the beans and corn to be tempted.

The path continued down the valley along the bank opposite the girls with the sheep and goats. Both shepherds, like Tarahumara women everywhere, wore full skirts with dozens of pleats in them, and full-sleeved blouses. Their skirts—and they may have been wearing more than one each—were maroon. One wore an orange print blouse while the other concealed her torso with a light red print blouse. The older of the two girls covered her long black hair with a blue scarf; her younger sister had nothing to hide her raven hair from the sun.

We continued until coming to a household next to the stream at the lower end of this part of the valley. Here were two log cabins and a wooden granary right next to one another. All three structures were well made, their corners locked by notches in the manner of toy Lincoln Logs. The planks used in their construction had been planed by an axe. The floor of the granary, like its ceiling, was made of carefully fitted boards. The dwellings had hard-packed earthen floors.

The granary had a clear space and wooden roof above its ceiling and a crawl space beneath the whole structure. Each dwelling had one rectangular doorway and no window; the granary had only a two-foot square door that could easily have been mistaken for a window. This particular door was latched with a padlock, but other granary doors

*Chicken coop, corral, and house*

30   Tarahumara

are latched with ingenious wooden locks with grooves and tumblers that can be opened only with a specially designed wooden key.

The roof of the granary sloped in a single plane from front to rear and extended beyond all four walls. In contrast, the roof of each dwelling was pitched in two directions from a center beam elevated at right angles to the length of the structure. There was no ceiling. Some of the roofing timbers were planks, but most of them were *canoas*, peeled V-shaped logs with a center notch or groove running down the entire length. A roof likely not to leak at all consists of alternate canoas laid to overlap longitudinally with their grooves interlocked. The principle is identical to that for laying semi-cylindrical roofing tiles.

A Tarahumara calls his dwelling a *galíki;* his granary or corn house is his *dekóchi.* The two log dwellings just described were exceptionally well made, their builder a virtuoso with an axe. His attitudes about permanent living space perhaps were influenced by what he had seen of Mexican construction. Typical, however, was his nearly airtight granary. To lose the corn it contained to insects, rot, theft, or mildew is to lose one's livelihood for the year. Corn, as well as beans and other dried seeds kept in the granary, are the staff of Tarahumara life. To lose them either occasions undue dependence on relatives and neighbors or, worse yet, undue dependence on Mexican cash economy. The latter forces a man to leave home and to sell cheaply the only commodity he has in good supply, his labor. The alternatives are all undesirable—malnutrition, starvation, or accepting uncertain charity from non-Tarahumaras. It is better by far that the granaries be properly constructed and their life-sustaining contents carefully guarded. It is not only that corn and beans support the lives of individual Tarahumaras; they are the underpinning of the Tarahumara way of life. In that sense, a granary is more than a storage unit; it is the stronghold of Tarahumara culture.

There are variations on the architectural theme of Tarahumara granaries. Some have neither windows nor doors but have instead roofs of heavy *canoas* that have to be removed by pushing one or more of the ceiling boards in the right direction to open this Chinese puzzle-like box. In areas where timbers are hard to get, old style granaries made of uncoursed rocks mortared together with mud are still used. Such granaries, looking like oversized mud daubers' nests, are commonly found in rock shelters.

Cornhouses store more than corn and beans. In the early 1930s Robert Zingg inventoried the contents of a Tarahumara granary located on a mountain ridge south of the Río Urique, and besides corn, he found:

> . . . one rifle, one small basket of seed beans, one bottle of turpentine, one basket of suet, one basket of white seed wheat and another of red, one large basket of calabash seed, one basket of brome-grass seed for making tesgüino, *several rawhide thongs, one buckskin quiver with blue-and-red decorated arrows with iron points, one almanac, two candlesticks from the church (for safekeeping), one large basket of wool,*

*one of the small "boiling pots" in which the mother ferment for* tesgüino *is made, a double-weave twilled basket and a hat, secured from the Indians of the gorges in trade.*

Nearly a half-century later, the contents of granaries are much the same. In addition to corn, whatever is particularly prized by its owner is securely put away in these structures. We saw a framed photograph of a group of Tarahumaras in one granary. Its owner was one of the men in the picture.

There is much greater architectural variation in houses than in granaries. According to Robert Zingg, the type most common in the sierra, more so than tightly constructed log cabins, is made by placing four four-foot-high notched uprights in holes dug with an iron bar. These are from ten to fifteen feet apart and form the corners of a square or rectangle. They are joined in pairs by two long V-shaped canoas. Two longer forked trunks about seven feet high are placed between the four corner posts. These support the ridge beam.

The roof boards for one side are measured so they slope exactly from the ridge beam at the top to the canoa below. They are overlaid in a double covering so that the roof will not leak.

The boards for the other side of the roof are measured longer, so that in sloping up from the canoa they project over the ridge beam, thus protecting the top of the house from leaks. This side of the roof also consists of a double overlaying course of boards.

The walls are merely long boards placed on edge beneath the canoas one above the other, to form the side from the ground to the gutter. These horizontal boards are held in place against the corner posts by means of two smaller uprights inside.

The back and front of this simple structure are finished by leaning boards of various lengths vertically against the open ends. Enough of them are cut to overlay one another,

*A homestead*

providing a fairly secure end. Entrance is gained by moving aside one or two boards.

The side walls of some houses are made of stone rather than of horizontal boards. These can be stones shaped into blocks with an axe and mortared together, rocks chinked together with mud, rocks tightly piled, or some combination of these. In parts of the mountains there are Tarahumara houses built entirely of chiseled stone blocks or of sun-dried adobe bricks.

In most houses, cooking or heating fires send smoke through the eaves or the slot along the ridge beam. Soot and smoke cause little concern among the Tarahumaras. In one house we saw soot hanging down from the inside of the roof and beams in the shape of foot-long black stalactites. In other houses, however, there are various kinds of fireplaces, flues, and homemade chimneys, some of stacked bottomless earthenware pots.

The simplest house of all consists of two upright forked poles connected by a single crossbeam against one or both sides of which vertical planks are laid. The end result is a wooden lean-to or tent whose front or rear can be closed merely by leaning more vertical planks against them. Tarahumaras also add usable floor space to already-standing structures by leaning planks against upright walls.

Two facts are clear. The first is that Tarahumaras are much more concerned about their granaries than their houses, with the amount of effort and skill involved in their construction being accordingly disproportionate. The second is that the Tarahumara house reflects a quite different set of values and concerns than our own with respect to such matters as permanency, privacy, status, and wealth. We expect our houses to be permanent; we expect them to protect their valued contents from the elements as well as from theft; we expect them to shield private activities from the inspection of outsiders; we acknowledge that they are a symbol of our social and economic status within the community.

Tarahumara houses, on the other hand, are temporary. A person may have one at his rancho and another near his fields. If he is used to moving from the high country to low country and back again on a seasonal basis, he might also have a rock shelter down in the barrancas he can call home. Should someone die in a house, formal tradition demands that the house be destroyed, although sometimes the custom is either ignored or a shaman is called in to perform a ceremony that will eliminate the need to dismantle the structure.

Anthropologist John Kennedy points out that Tarahumaras do not separate their daily lives in terms of "indoors" and "outdoors." Their use of space is flexible. Cooking, sleeping, making baskets, shaping pots, eating, fornicating, drinking, loafing—these are things that can be done outside of houses as well as inside them. If warmth is provided by a fire, four walls, and a roof, so can it be provided by an outdoor fire, heavy wool blanket, and extra skirts. One can sleep where one becomes sleepy. There are no soft mattresses or cots in Tarahumara houses, only plaited mats, skins, or hard wooden boards for lying upon, none of them necessarily more comfortable than the ground outside.

Because Tarahumara houses typically have no windows, they are dark inside, illuminated by daylight penetrating an open door or numerous cracks in the walls or roof. Furnishings—as likely to be found outside as inside—are the epitome of simplicity. They

include a stone metate and mano for grinding corn and other foods; several plaited baskets, most commonly the bowl-shaped *guari*; a few earthenware cooking and eating pots as well as some *tesgüino* jars; tin cans; a bucket or two; some half gourd shells; four or five sleeping boards; and perhaps a bow and arrows, violin, gourd rattles, hide drum, or guitar. Clothing and blankets may be here or stored in the granary or elsewhere.

Every living site must have at least one metate and mano; most have more than one set. Except for these heavy objects, most possessions are easily carried from place to place. Even large *tesgüino* jars can be transported by wrapping them in a blanket.

A Tarahumara's wealth and his community standing are not measured by the numbers of his material possessions, although rich men are likely to have excellent blankets and their wives new skirts and blouses which they sew themselves. They may also own a greater variety of goods. But the real measure of a person's industry, common sense, organizational skill, and technical know-how—all qualities greatly admired by Tarahumaras and likely to give their possessor high status within the community—is the num-

*Tarahumara*   35

*Maria Teresa Borja*

ber of his granaries, the number of his acres, the numbers of his livestock, and the numbers of times he has been willing to give food to those who ask for it. In short, the ability to produce food and share it provides the definition of Tarahumara success. Land, livestock, granaries, and institutionalized generosity are ultimately linked in the arena of subsistence. Houses and wealth measured in terms of accumulated artifacts have little bearing on the matter of whether one eats or not.

None of this is to suggest that Tarahumaras are not influenced by their Mexican neighbors. The introduction of the steel axe by Spaniards brought about a minor revolution in Tarahumara architecture. Log cabins, granaries, and other wooden structures are virtually impossible to make without axes. The prehistoric stone axe was suitable only for felling trees, inefficiently at best. Pre-Spanish architecture consisted chiefly of caves and structures of stones, mud, and brush.

The steel axe made possible boards, canoes, and notched logs. Tarahumaras had before them the models of Spanish and Mexican architecture, even as they do today. Thus it is that houses of squared stones, sun-dried adobe bricks, and tightly constructed log walls are included in the modern Tarahumara inventory. Who can say, moreover, there are not now permanently settled Tarahumaras who, like Mexicans, have come to think of a house as a symbol of wealth and prestige? It would be strange were it otherwise.

Back along the stream, we stood hesitantly outside the houses at the lower end of the valley. Very shortly a man came out of one of the two dwellings, smiling, and we were put at ease. He extended a right hand to each of us in turn, and we barely touched the insides of all four fingers. That is a Tarahumara "handshake." He said, as did we,

*Tarahumara* 37

"*Kwira bá.*" The shortened form is *kwirá.* It is a greeting believed to come from the Spanish *cuidar* (to look after, to care, to heed) or *cuidado* (care, keeping). In English it conveys the sense of "Good morning," "Good day," or "Good evening."

"*¿Usted es Francisco?*" I asked.

"*Sí,*" was the reply.

"*Soy un amigo de Edmundo,*" I explained. And pointing up the valley, "*Edmundo esta allá. El va venir. ¿Comprende usted?*"

"*Sí,*" Francisco answered. "*Yo comprendo.*"

Our Spanish was poor, mine more than his, but we found ourselves speaking the same language: poor Spanish. We soon satisfied ourselves that we understood one another, whether we did or not.

Virtually all Tarahumaras who continue to think of themselves as Tarahumaras (Rarámuri) speak only their own language in everyday discourse. Nearly all of them are bilingual in Tarahumara and Spanish to varying degrees. Some of them—especially those who have spent time in mission boarding schools—are fluent in both tongues. Tarahumara is a Uto-Aztecan language, closely related to the Warihio language spoken in Sonora and elsewhere in Chihuahua. It is more distantly related to Cáhita, the language of the Yaqui and Mayo Indians of Sonora and Sinaloa. Cáhita and Tarahumara are no more mutually intelligible than English and Dutch.

Still more distantly related to Tarahumara, but related nonetheless, is a whole series of Piman languages: Northern Tepehuane, Southern Tepehuane, Tepecano, two Lower Pima dialects, Papago, and Gila River Pima. These are spoken to the south, west, and northwest of the Sierra Tarahumara. Indeed, Uto-Aztecan languages are in use all the way from Wyoming and southern Idaho to northern Nicaragua.

That his language has such a distinguished lineage and is so widespread was of no moment to our new acquaintance, who was dressed in traditional Tarahumara male garb. He struck a handsome, short-statured pose in his bright red headband, its two tails descending down his back to his hips; his single-piece, embroidered white loincloth worn square across the rear and tied around his waist with a beautifully woven and decorated woolen sash, the same kind worn as belts by the women; his full-sleeved, short-waisted pullover blouse worn nearly out of sight beneath a white and embroidered *cotón,* a poncho-like garment historically woven out of wool to provide warmth but now sewn from plain coarse muslin; and his truck-tire sandals tied to his feet and ankles with leather thongs. Had it been winter he would have had a blanket wrapped around him, either one woven by a Tarahumara weaver or one acquired from a store in some Mexican settlement.

In some areas the men wear an additional piece of cloth around their waists, giving the effect of a two-piece loincloth. The second piece points toward the ground at the rear in a triangle. And from area to area there are different styles of embroidery, different ways of folding and wearing the headband (women wear them as well), different preferences in colors, and different degrees in the use of Mexican clothing. Mexican straw hats,

*Home on a rainy day*

trousers, shirts, coats, bandanas, and even shoes are commonly worn by Tarahumaras who live in close proximity to Mexican communities. It is ironic that sometimes genuinely wealthy Tarahumaras proudly wear cast-off Mexican or American clothes, looking utterly poverty-stricken, while genuinely poverty-stricken Tarahumaras who dress in clothing of their own fashion and manufacture look infinitely better off.

Photographs taken by Lumholtz in the 1890s show clearly that men used to wear woolen loincloths and the women wore woolen skirts, all of which they wove themselves. The woolen loincloths are gone and the skirts are all but a thing of the past. Likewise, the cotón or poncho-like garment, also worn by women but more commonly by men, is now muslin. If the Lumholtz pictures can be taken as representative, the long-tailed, two-tailed headband seems to have grown in popularity in the last ninety years, with a simple headband with short tails or no tails having been more common in the 1890s.

The French actor and theorist of drama, Antonin Artaud, visited the Tarahumaras in 1936. He was not impressed when Tarahumaras told him they wore headbands simply to hold their hair in place. He knew, even if they didn't, that they worshipped "a transcendent principle of Nature which is Male and Female . . . [a]nd they wear this principle on their heads like Pharaoh Initiates." For Artaud, if for no one else, the two tails or points on the headbands were sure evidence that the male and female principles of nature exist simultaneously within the Tarahumara race. "In short, he concluded, "they wear their philosophy on their heads, and this philosophy reconciles the influence of the two contrary forces in an equilibrium that partakes of the divine." Probably never before in history has the headband been asked to carry such a weighty philosophical load.

When Father Fonte first met the Tarahumaras in 1607 they made all of their clothing with the materials at hand, largely from plant fibers but no doubt from hides of wild animals as well. A short time after the introduction of sheep, and still in the seventeenth century, wool began to substitute for plant fiber, with the Tarahumaras, principally the women, weaving the wool and shaping the clothing. Precisely when Tarahumaras first began to acquire woven cotton cloth and other imported textiles is difficult to say, although the process doubtless began sometime in the 1600s. By the 1930s, most Tarahumara clothing was sewn from muslin and from other cloth manufactured elsewhere, but the sewing was done by the women. This continues today. Women enhance their sewing by doing lovely embroidery, chiefly on blouses, loincloths, and cotóns. The designs, in a full range of colors provided by commercial embroidery yarns, emphasize life forms: floral, human, and other animal, and include geometric figures which may represent such entities as the sun and moon. Embroidery is one of the more important Tarahumara art forms. Their embroidered designs have a charm and naiveté that are unique.

Having exhausted our vocabulary of mutually intelligible words, our new acquaintance took his leave of us, disappearing inside his house while we were left to sit on rocks in the narrow streak of shade provided by the overhanging eaves of his dwelling. In time he reemerged, accompanied by his young son. The two of them climbed to a rock high on the mountain slope above their valley where they had a clear view of the trails coming down from above. They were going to sit and wait for the appearance of our mutual friend.

We walked around, sat, napped, took pictures. Small white clouds grew larger against the blue sky, and their numbers increased. The air was neither too warm nor too cold. A small side stream coming into the valley behind the house joined the main stream just below it. The corn and beans formed solid swatches of green along the stream's edge. The girls and the dogs continued to move the sheep and goats from here to there. It was a symphony pastorale, a wholly idyllic rural scene: shepherds and their flock, water and ripening crops; green, blue, brown, and white, punctuated by red blouses, skirts, and headband.

A short distance upslope from where we chose to rest for a while there was a simple log corral of poles about twelve feet long, cribbed together to form a square. No corner posts tied adjacent sides. Poles, five on each side, were merely stacked one over the other. The corral rested in a cleared area next to two square patches of darkened ground. The effect from a distance was that of checkered squares. Next year's fields were already being prepared with fertilizer, the gift of goats and sheep.

"In a very real sense," wrote Robert Zingg, "the Tarahumara lives on the sparse grass of the mountainside, collected for him by the animals and transformed through the cycle of animal food to a fertilizer for the corn which is the staff of Tarhumara life. This is the most elaborate, delicate, and laborious adjustment of culture to natural environment in their ecology."

The wonder is that Tarahumaras seldom eat the meat of any of their livestock, cattle included. Animals are killed and their meat eaten on ceremonial occasions, such as during important religious fiestas, but, with the possible exception of pigs, which are eaten, their paramount role in Tarahumara life is to provide fertilizer for the fields. Sheep give up their wool for blankets, sashes, and ribbons; oxen pull wooden plows; horses and burros—not common animals in the Sierra Tarahumara—are ridden and used as beasts of burden. All livestock are a walking savings account, potential commodities that can be sold or traded in time of need as a hedge against starvation. But it is their manure that endears them to these gentle mountain farmers.

Tarahumaras who have oxen and cows keep them penned at night in sturdier corrals than those erected for sheep and goats. The animals are shepherded about during the day by children, young women, and dogs; at night they are kept penned up, either in a corral or in a cave or rock shelter. The "roving corral" system of fertilizing the fields is an effective and ingenious one; it is much easier to move the corrals from time to time than it is to carry large quantities of manure to the fields. However, the people can and do haul fertilizer considerable distances. It is often carried down from rock shelters where livestock have been penned up or from more permanent corrals erected near people's houses. Manure can be packed in old blankets, skirts or other cloth, hides, or in large gunny sacks. In one place we watched a man shovel manure from a corral into a huge gunny sack until the sack weighed more than 100 pounds, hoist the sack onto his back, carry it about 500

*Marcos and his violin*

yards to his field, empty the contents and walk back to the corral to repeat the process. He made possibly as many as a hundred such trips.

The fields themselves are situated on land as rich in soil and as free of rocks as people can make them. The rocks are stacked into mile upon mile of thick walls three, four, and even five feet high. Some such walls, separating livestock from fields and demarcating the limits of ranchos and pueblos, are straight-sided works of geometric art. The amount of patient and back-breaking labor that has gone into them is incalculable. If good walls do indeed make good neighbors, parts of the eastern Sierra Tarahumara, especially, must be inhabited by the best neighbors in the world. In the meantime, thousands of acres have thus become rock-free farm lands.

Although fields vary in size, it has been estimated that to survive at a subsistence level there must be about one-quarter acre cultivated per person, including children, so that a family of five would need to have a one and one-quarter acre farm. However, since most farms depend on direct rainfall and since Tarahumaras do not irrigate their fields, more cultivated acreage would provide insurance against the inevitable bad years when rainfall is insufficient. In a few areas in the Sierra Tarahumara there are fields planted in the floodplains of rivers such that the crops can get water even in the absence of direct rainfall, but such acreage is the exception rather than the rule. In pre-Spanish times, the opposite may have been true.

Corn, squash, and beans, the great triumvirate of American Indian cultivated crops, were and are the staples in Tarahumara diet, with corn the most important. Fertilized fields are plowed in late February or in March, oxen pulling a wooden plow attached to a wooden yoke designed to space the furrows such that the ground beneath the growing cornstalks can later be cultivated by oxen and plow. This first plowing involves two passes in a crisscross pattern. By walking one of the oxen in a previously made furrow, all the furrows can be kept parallel. Plowing is to a depth of about five or six inches.

*Tarahumara* 43

*Cultivating the cornfield*

44   Tarahumara

Sometimes, after the second plowing, it is necessary to run a drag over the fields to break up large clods. The homemade drag, like the plow, is pulled by oxen hitched to a yoke. If the dragging takes place, the field must be plowed a third time.

Corn is seeded in April or May, depending on the particular location, before the onset of a hoped-for short rainy season. April, May, and June are crucial in the life of growing corn. Sufficient rain is needed to insure eventual maturity. Men and boys shouldering bags filled with seed corn walk along the furrows to plant with digging sticks. They poke a three-inch hole into the earth at every step and press the stick to hold the hole open while three or four seeds are expertly dropped into it. The planter removes the stick without pausing, covers the seeded hole with his foot, and repeats the process, moving steadily forward.

When the corn is a few inches high, Tarahumaras cultivate the fields with a wooden-handled iron hoe. This is done as often as necessary to rid the fields of weeds before the stalks are high enough to make it possible to cultivate with oxen and plow. In June or July, with the corn about two feet high, a hoe is used to work the earth at the base of each stalk into a mound. Tarahumaras believe this will make the corn grow faster and prevent the stalks from being blown over or washed away in a flood.

By August the corn has begun to flower and the ears have formed. This is none too soon, because granaries are getting dangerously low. During September the ears fill out. Some green corn may be picked, but the real harvest waits until early November when mature ears are pulled from the stalks by hand, shucked with the aid of a small peg of wood lashed to the hand, and tossed into a specially made burden basket. The corn will be carried to a wooden platform to dry for two or three weeks before it is stored in the granary. If there is no wooden corn-drying platform, the freshly picked ears are spread on a rocky floor inside a stone or log corral where they are covered with boards and guarded from animals twenty-four hours a day.

Six different major races of corn *(Zea mays)*, as well as some minor races, are grown among the Tarahumara. These include popcorn, sweet corn, roasting-ear corn, and flint corn; kernels are shades of white, yellow, red, or black (dark blue). Some ears have more than one color of kernel.

Corn is eaten by Tarahumaras mainly in the form of *pinole*, tortillas, *esquiate, atole,* tamales, and boiled and roasted ears. It is probably not too much of an exaggeration to suggest that everything that can be done with corn to make it edible is done by Tarahumaras; their list of corn recipes is seemingly limitless. And most important of all, perhaps, they drink it in the form of corn beer, their famed (or infamous) *tesgüino (suguiki* in their own language).

There are parts of the agricultural cycle, including the initial preparation of fields, planting, and possibly fencing that can often be better accomplished with large work crews. Moreover, if one does not have oxen and is forced to borrow them, the animals' owner will probably provide his services as well. Such communal work gatherings, analogous to the "working bees" of the Anglo-American western frontier, may also take place at the building of a granary or house, the repair of a church or "courthouse," or on any other occasion when many people can do a better job than a few. Such gatherings, as well as those for either native or Catholic religious observances (discounting regular Tarahumara attendance at church in pueblos where there are missionaries) invariably take place with the help of a *tesgüinada,* or Tarahumara-style beer bust.

It would be almost impossible to overstate the importance of corn beer and corn beer parties in the lives of Tarahumaras. Anthropologist John Kennedy, who has given more objective consideration to the institution of the tesgüinada than anyone else, estimates that each adult spends about 100 days out of each year, or more than a fourth of his time, directly involved in the preparation, consumption, and recovery from the effects of this national drink.

The corn beer party is certainly a very old institution in the Sierra Tarahumara, possibly pre-Spanish. The early Jesuits and virtually all of the missionaries since the seventeenth century have regarded it as an evil, although modern missionaries are likely to be more tolerant of the custom than their colonial predecessors.

Historian Peter Dunne recounts the visit of two Jesuit missionaries to a Tarahumara settlement late in 1675 or early in 1676. The padres, who had been invited to the community, were received with a warm and joyous welcome by the natives.

> *But something discouraging transpired. The fathers learned that the inhabitants . . . had gathered together a great quantity of their strong liquor [most probably tesgüino]. That very night they had planned a carousal to celebrate the coming of the Black Robes [i.e., Jesuits]. The missionaries objected strongly. They declared they would not have entered the pueblo had they known this was to be the outcome. It was not their intention, they said, to encourage by their presence such offenses against God as drunkenness. Sorry, it was too late to change their plans, replied the Indians. Guests had been invited from all around; the liquor had been collected. The fathers could not this time dissuade them from the drunken celebration they had fixed their minds upon.*
>
> *Realizing to what extremes of ferocious passion the drunken savage can be led, the two Jesuits dared not spend the night in this strange place. Collecting what things were immediately necessary they secretly made their way out of the pueblo after dark and clambered up to a rocky ledge, which they hoped the intoxicated Indians would not be able to reach. They were right on both counts. Near midnight the Indians went to the hut looking for them and finding the padres had fled ransacked the dwelling from top to bottom. The fathers high on their ledge were not molested, and if the howling and the crying of the intoxicated ceased in the early hours of the morning the missionaries might have been able to snatch a few winks of sleep.*
>
> *[Finally, some of the Indians climbed to the missionaries' perch to indicate] that the [Tarahumaras] were now sober and since the padres had come so far to baptize them why did they not start at once? It was a good time to begin, for many bags and jugs of liquor, the envoys said, had been left untouched for a still greater celebration.*

What really happens at a tesgüinada, at least at one held in the twentieth century, is not likely to be quite so bad as the two seventeenth century Jesuits imagined. Fights are known to occur at Tarahumara beer parties. Indeed, they are virtually the only occasion at which fighting is permitted. But "ferocious passions" are not the kinds of passions typically unleashed, and murder or serious maiming are very, very rare.

In its simplest, most classic form, tesgüino is a fermented drink made year around from sprouted corn. Variants are also made from the still-green stalks of roasting-ear corn, from the baked hearts of several species of *Agave*, from the hearts of sotol, from the fruit of certain cactuses, shrubs, and trees, including peaches. Even wheat is converted into tesgüino.

The process is begun by malting the corn. From fifteen to forty-five pounds of corn are spread in shallow baskets set in a dark corner of the house where light will not reach. This will make from fifteen to fifty gallons of tesgüino. The basket is covered with pine needles or grass and the baskets are sprinkled each day for four or five days. If the corn being sprouted is a hard, flint corn, it may first be moistened and kept wet in a sack or basket inside an earthenware jar set in a warm place.

The corn is kept moist until it sprouts. Should it germinate in sunlight, the sprouts will be green and bitter. White sprouts produce sweet tesgüino.

By the time the sprouts are a little more than an inch long, the starch in the corn has been converted into fermentable sugars. It is removed from the baskets and mashed or ground two or three times on a metate. The mashed sprouts are placed in a large pottery jar with plenty of water and boiled for eight hours or so. Now it is common to see corn beer being boiled in metal containers instead of in ceramic *ollas* (pottery jars).

When the boiling brew turns yellowish, it is taken from the fire and cooled. The cooled liquid is run through a basketry strainer into another olla.

At this point different herbs are ground with water to make a sticky paste. The paste is mixed with more water in small, special fermenting pots called *sikolí donéla*, "boiling pot," by the Tarahumaras. The most popular catalyst is the crushed, dried stem of *basiáwi*, or brome grass (*Bromus* sp.). The fruiting head of this plant can also be used, as can parts of eight or nine other plants. The fermenting pots have in their pores an inoculant which introduces some kinds of microorganisms into the mixture. These pots are never washed and are used solely in the fermentation process. Tarahumaras say they have "learned to boil [i.e., ferment] well from each other." To start a new fermentation pot, old tesgüino, large amounts of brome grass paste, or even baby fecal matter in maize solution can be allowed to soak in it.

When the fermenting pot is filled, it is set in a warm place near the fire and allowed to ferment all night. The next morning its contents are mixed with the strained corn liquid, the jars are covered, and the beer is allowed to ferment for another three or four days. Then it is time for the beer party to begin. Moreover, it should begin at once, because tesgüino can spoil within twelve to twenty-four hours. If fifty gallons have been prepared, then fifty gallons must be drunk. What could be worse than wasting all the effort that has gone into its preparation, not to mention the forty-five pounds of corn kernels?

If a man has a field to be cleared and prepared for planting, he sends out word to neighboring ranchos letting all the adults know they are being invited to a tesgüinada. They arrive at the appointed time, knowing full well that in return for their labor in helping prepare someone else's field they will be rewarded with a beer party. They may work all day, drink all night, recover in the morning, and finish up the work the next afternoon. Except that mothers sometimes come to tesgüinadas bringing their infants with them, there are no children present. To be old enough to drink tesgüino is to be old enough to accept full adult responsibilities. The girls must be of childbearing age; the boys must be old enough to be thought of as men. While a tesgüinada is in progress, children tend the flocks and keep the home fires burning.

Carl Lumholtz took part in numerous tesgüinadas during his stay in the Sierra Tara-humara in the 1890s. His description of them, just as apropos today, is probably a little more objective than that of the seventeenth-century Jesuits who refused to become involved. Says Lumholtz:

> . . . *Little or nothing of the tesvino is spared, and it is the avowed intention and aim of everybody to get "a beautiful intoxication." They all like to get drunk. An Indian explained to me that the drunken people weep with delight, because they are so perfectly happy. . . .*
>
> *But unfortunately this blissful stage of their intoxication does not last long, and then the animal nature in them manifests itself. Under the influence of the liquor, men and women rapidly lose that bashfulness and modesty which in ordinary life are such characteristic traits of their deportment. Furthermore, whatever grudge one man may have against another now crops out, and very likely a fight will ensue, in which the two opponents recklessly pull each other's hair and punch each other's faces. Sometimes in such an outbreak of unreasoning animalism one of the combatants will seize a stone and batter the other one's head to crush it. Afterward, when sober again, the murderer may deeply deplore his deed—if he remembers it at all.*
>
> *Mothers, when overcome by the spirit of the feast, may unawares allow their babies to fall out of the blankets and into the fire. Children may frequently be seen with bruises and scars which they carry as mementoes of some tesvino feast. I know of one man who had no hair on one side of his head, having when a child been a victim of such an accident. But seldom, if ever, is a child allowed to become fatally injured.*
>
> *Taking it all in all, it is a good-natured, jolly, silly crowd, out for a good time and enjoying themselves. All are good friends, and familiarity becomes unlimited. Late in the afternoon those still able to walk start on their way home. Rarely, however, can they reach their domiciles, if these are any distance off, before nature enforces her rights; and the track is strewn with men and women, who, overcome with the effects of their spree, have lain down wherever they happened to be, to sleep themselves sober. Tarahumare society has not yet advanced far enough to see anything disgraceful in debauches of this kind, which, if viewed from their standpoint, are* pro bono publico; *and we ourselves need go back only to our grandfathers' and great-grandfathers' time to find that inebriety was not at all inconsistent with good morals and high standing. Moreover, no matter how often the Tarahumares indulge in such saturnalia, as soon as they recover their senses they are as decorous and solemn as ever. Their native stimulant does not seem to affect either their physical or their mental faculties, and, all scientific theories to the contrary, their children are strong, healthy, and bright.*
>
> *Aside from social and religious considerations, the drinking of tesvino is a vital factor in the national life of the tribe. Incredible as it may sound, yet, after prolonged and careful research into this interesting psy-*

*chological problem, I do not hesitate to state that in the ordinary course
of his existence the uncivilised Tarahumare is too bashful and modest to
enforce his matrimonial rights and privileges; and that by means of tes-
vino chiefly the race is kept alive and increasing. It is especially at the
feasts connected with the agricultural work that sexual promiscuity
takes place.*

While it may be asking too much of the tesgüinada to insist that it is the only occasion during which men have intercourse with their wives, John G. Kennedy, who studied
the tesgüinada more than fifty years after Lumholtz wrote his account, agrees that *"tesgüino* serves as a lubricant of social interaction, enabling the Tarahumaras to temporarily overcome their fears of others in order to engage in needed sociality."

In Kennedy's view, the institution of the tesgüinada is so important to the social
fabric of Tarahumara culture that what he calls the *"tesgüino* network" actually constitutes "the major structural form of the Tarahumara social system above the family and
residence group."

To put the matter more simply, the basic unit of Tarahumara culture is the family-
household unit. Beyond that is the cluster of such units that make up a rancho, a place
with fields and a name. Next is the group of people who customarily drink together at
beer parties. They come from several communities, not merely from one rancho or pueblo.

Given the scattered nature of Tarahumara settlements and the extreme isolation of
people from one another, beer parties hosted by different households in different ranchos
bring about many positive benefits for the people, economic, religious, and social. There
are many times annually in the lives of Tarahumaras that there simply are not enough of
them in a household or rancho to carry out certain essential tasks. Most of these are related to agriculture, but they can involve any major, heavy construction as well, such as
building houses, granaries, corn-drying platforms, and large fences or corrals. The tesgüinada is the catalyst which brings people together into an effective work force.

There are other important occasions for tesgüinadas. Considering the vagaries of
weather, especially in terms of needed rainfall, and the fact that Tarahumaras, like everyone else in the world, suffer illnesses and occasional epidemic disease, it is not surprising
that they have evolved ritualized means of coping with these ever-potential problems.
And again, recalling their scattered settlement pattern, neither is it surprising they have
chosen to participate in these religious rituals collectively. Diseases and droughts are
threats to the lives of everyone, not merely to members of an isolated household.

So it is that curing ceremonies, like working bees, call for tesgüinadas. It should be
pointed out that in addition to individual human beings, animals and fields of crops can
also be "cured." Native curing fiestas are held as well for the prevention of sickness; for
the bringing of rain; to accompany birth and death; to "cure" first corn, beans, and other
crops. Anthropologist Wendell Bennett rather cynically observes, "As in many of these
smaller *fiestas,* in which the main purpose is to eat meat and to drink, any excuse is given
for its performance."

A great many such curing fiestas, since they involve rain, fields, and crops, take
place between the March preparation of fields and the November harvest. Those involv-

ing birth, death, and sick animals and human beings take place as needed. The chief religious practitioners in such fiestas are the shaman and the chanters. The shaman, curer, or native ritual specialist—however one chooses to label him—is a person with supernatural power. It is his job to diagnose and to cure. The chanters, on the other hand, are ordinary Tarahumaras who have learned the proper chants and rhythms to go along with the curing ceremonies. Their musical instrument is a special gourd rattle, and their presence is essential at all native rituals requiring dancing. However, chanters do not cure; neither do shamans chant.

Curing rituals normally take place at a cleared, flat area found near every Tarahumara household. This dancing place, or "dance patio" as it has come to be known in English, is where a goat or cow later to be served at the feast is sacrificed. It is where ceremonies are carried out and where ritual dancing will occur. Before a curing fiesta three crosses are erected at the eastern edge of the dance patio. A ceremonial table or wooden altar is set up on the west side of the crosses, crosses which Lumholtz said represented Father Sun, Mother Moon, and Morning Star. The ceremonial table is stacked with baskets and pottery bowls filled with such things as pinole (ground parched corn), tortillas, tamales, and the boiled meat of whatever animal or animals have been sacrificed. In addition to goats and cattle, sheep, chickens, burros, mules, horses, deer, and squirrels may provide meat for a fiesta diet.

These offerings are meant for Father God, referred to by Tarahumaras either as *Tata Dios* or *Onorúame*. It is put there for him to enjoy its essence by smelling it before it is eaten by the people. Ollas of tesgüino are placed behind the crosses. There is also an offering in a piece of broken pottery under the table for *El Diablo*. It consists of worthless food scraps, such as peach pits, and is put there to keep El Diablo from helping himself to the food put out for Tata Dios. Additional ollas of tesgüino are kept in private houses by individuals.

The shaman dedicates the tesgüino in household ollas; a chanter dedicates that kept behind the crosses. The ceremonies begin when the chanters shake their rattles and chant songs with unintelligible words. Their knees move slightly, keeping time with the chanting. The women rise and dance to the accompaniment of the complicated rhythms. The chants and the dances are short, but are repeated at intervals again and again throughout the night. It is the chanting that is essential; it continues whether there is dancing or not. This dance by the women accompanied by male chanters is called the *yúmari* dance. It always takes place on the patio in front of the altar and crosses.

Toward morning, and before the feasting and drinking start, the men and women dance together in a very fast dance called the *dutubúri*. At dawn, the food is eaten and drinking commences. With some ceremonies, there may be yet another yúmari dance.

In addition to the native shamans and chanters who take part in such ceremonies, there also may be male *matachine* dancers, fiddlers, and guitar players, or Pharisee drummers and flute players. These are people important in the observance of Christian feasts. They perform to one side of the main dance patio.

If tesgüinadas function in the economic and religious realms of Tarahumara society, so are they of enormous psychological importance to the people in attendance. They pro-

*Tarahumara* 51

*Blessing the food*

52    Tarahumara

*Yúmari chanter*

vide an outlet for sex, including extramarital sex; they afford the opportunity for people to release pent-up aggressions; they serve as a reminder that one has a wide circle of friends on whom one can rely; they help obviate the loneliness which would otherwise go along with the people's extreme physical isolation from one another; and, not the least of all, they provide plenty of fun. If the Rarámuri had not taken the name of "foot runners" for themselves, they would probably have become known as the "tesgüino drinkers." It is no wonder that neither Jesuits nor anyone else has succeeded in suppressing such a fine old custom.

For all of the prodigious quantities of beer that are consumed, Tarahumaras have not become alcoholics. Kennedy suggests this is because the alcoholic content of the beer is relatively low; it is expensive in terms of corn used; and it has to be drunk at once because it cannot be stored. Above all, perhaps, it is a group social activity rather than an individual affair. "It therefore does not produce the bizarre pathology of Western alcoholism."

Corn is not all Tarahumaras eat and drink. Meat, including fish, chickens, squirrels, and domestic animals killed on ceremonial occasions, probably constitutes less than five percent of the diet. Even so, it is not correct to say that Tarahumaras are vegetarians. It is simply that meat is not among their preferred foods.

Next to corn, beans are the most important cultivated crop. They raise several varieties of the common bean, largely small vine or bush forms, but including one variety of pole bean. Chili may rank third in importance as a crop, followed by squash, three species in all. Although only one species of chili peppers is used, there are four types, including the wild *chili piquín* or *chiltipín*. The *chiltipín* is by far the hottest of the chilis, certain to add flame to any dish in which it is served. Tarahumaras add chili to all bean, corn, and meat dishes when they have it, and it supplies important nutritive elements as well as the hot, penetrating flavor for which chilis are famous.

In the eastern part of the Sierra Tarahumara these crops are grown either in the floodplains of rivers, where they are likely to be fertilized by animal manure carried to them, or in fields fertilized via the "moving corral" method, called *barbecho* in Spanish.

On the slopes of the upper barrancas, *milpa* or slash-and-burn agriculture is the rule. The oaks are cut in November and December and allowed to dry in the longitudinal rows where they have been stacked. The dry brush stems are burned in May. When the rains come in June seeds are planted in the ash-covered earth with the help of a digging stick. Such fields produce only for two or three years before they have to be given a five to ten year rest.

Finally, there is also terrace or *trinchera* agriculture in which stone walls are used to form terraced slopes on the sides of hills or mountains. The runoff from rains in addition to the forces of wind and gravity bring about a buildup of soil in the terraced plots. While such fields are not terribly productive, they can be used for a few years before they have to be abandoned.

Corn, beans, chili, and squash are a remarkably nutritionally sound diet. Corn and beans are high in protein; the amino acids scarce in corn are present in beans. Moreover, the way in which Tarahumaras prepare corn to make tortillas and tamales considerably enhances the amount of protein, amino acids, and niacin available for human digestion. Tarahumaras boil corn with lime or ashes to prepare *nixtamal*, the dough ingredient for their tamales and tortillas. This alkalai process makes it much more nutritious.

Chilis are a rich source of vitamins A and C; squashes provide carbohydrates, calcium, phosphorus, iron, thiamine, riboflavin, niacin, and vitamins A and C.

Tarahumaras also rely heavily on the collecting of potherbs, known as a group as *quelites*. These are green weeds and more than a dozen kinds are gathered. Two kinds, *Brassica* and *Lepidium*, are raised as garden crops in addition to being collected in the wild. In spite of the fact that these plants offer a rich source of vitamins C and A and calcium as well as important amounts of thiamine and riboflavin, younger Tarahumaras are being pressured by their more "progressive" neighbors to give up "weeds" in favor of processed foods. Nonetheless, the Tarahumara diet remains dependent on quelites.

Onions are gathered wild and occasionally grown as garden crops. Chilis, *cilantro*, and a turnip-like plant are also grown in small gardens.

The fruits, herbage, nuts, seeds, and roots of hundreds of different wild plants are collected in their place and season. Occasionally flies, grasshoppers, locusts, caterpillars, and various insect larvae are toasted on coals and eaten. Tarahumaras also gather wild honey and eat tadpoles and various kinds of lizards. In areas where they can be grown, cherries, wild plums, mulberries, peaches, apples, crab apples, pomegranates, quinces, apricots, and pears are propagated. Oranges, avocados, and lemons are grown in the lowlands. It is common to see fruit trees with their trunks protected from livestock by a circle of boards leaned against them.

Robert Bye, a botanist who has made intensive studies of the Tarahumara use of plants, tells us they employ at least 294 different plants from 77 plant families for medical purposes. More than 41 kinds of plants from Tarahumara country have been counted in the herb markets of Ciudad Chihuahua and Juárez, evidence of the thriving Tarahumara trade in medicinal plants. In each area of the Sierra there is usually a *yerbero*, a person who goes out of his way to collect plants for city markets. Other people simply collect them so that when they go to the city they will be able to earn a few pesos. In any case, for nearly a century it is certain that herbs have provided one of the thin strands linking Tarahumaras to Mexico's cash economy.

Probably fewer than one percent of the Tarahumaras actively partake of peyote, a generic term for hallucinatory cactuses, especially *Lophophora williamsii*. Its ritual consumption is largely confined to one small region of the Sierra Tarahumara, but certain writers—most notably Antonin Artaud—have exaggerated its extent and left readers with the impression that peyote use is widespread among Tarahumaras. Lengthy published discussions of hallucinatory plants more accurately reflect the fascination these have held for authors than their actual importance among Indians. One is reminded of the overemphasis in print on the snake dance of the Hopi Indians. The thousands of words written on the subject are totally out of proportion to its meaning in Hopi ceremonialism.

It is not that Tarahumaras lack knowledge of and respect for narcotic cactuses and herbs. Plants capable of altering the senses are used for ritual and medicinal purposes, but Tarahumaras traditionally fear them. Ritual requirements and taboos greatly restrict their use.

No one has yet made a serious inventory of the non-native foods in the Tarahumaras' modern diet. The closer one lives to a store the more likely the diet is to be supplemented with processed foods. Salt is supplied from the outside world, and, in spite of the fact that tobacco is locally cultivated in gardens, most cigarettes are bought in stores. Tarahumaras love to smoke and they prefer manufactured and packaged cigarettes to their home grown and homemade kind.

Canned goods, dried fruits, and such items as rice and instant spaghetti and macaroni are commonly seen around Tarahumara houses. So are lard buckets and aerosol cans of insecticides, including repellents. Corn, squash, beans, and chili, however, remain the staples in the diet, and even were the amenities of store-bought foods to disappear, one has the feeling Tarahumaras would continue to get along in their mountain fastness just as they have for the past 350 years. They are involved in the Mexican economy; most of them do not yet appear to be dependent on it.

The afternoon sun bore down, its heat relieved when clouds, gathering in greater numbers, cast wide shadows. We climbed the slope opposite the house and stretched out under a couple of pine trees to wait for our absent friend. Across the valley, and a little higher upslope, our new Tarahumara acquaintance could be seen easily. A striking figure in his white cotón and loincloth and red headband, he alternately stood and sat on a rock, always looking up the valley where he would be able to see our friend. His son chose to lie in the shade of a tree near his father; the print blouse he wore blended in more readily with the background.

Toward mid-afternoon, our friend suddenly and unexpectedly arrived at the house. He had taken a longer trail over the mountains and had not come down the main valley trail. All of us converged at the house; our friend talked in Spanish and Tarahumara to the head of the household, and we were all invited inside for the first time. The man's wife sat on a plaited mat on the dirt floor. At our request she showed us some of the clothes she had embroidered. She is an artist with needle and thread. It turned out she is also an artist of another kind. Here and there on the outside of the family granary and house she had used chalk or some kind of white rock to draw figures of people, Tarahumaras in their native costumes. The drawings of men, women, and children were stylized, but the attire—full skirts, headbands, and loincloths—was unmistakable. In a different setting such drawings would be called "graffiti." Here, it was distinctly folk art. She had a blue pencil, and I persuaded her to use it to draw a man, woman, and girl in my notebook.

We took our leave. The three of us, reunited after having parted ways at the summit, continued down the stream toward its junction with a major river. The valley below the house quickly pinched down into a canyon again, only to open soon into another valley wide enough to support more plots of corn and beans. Where this valley opened, perched on the slope to the left, were two traditional board- and canoa-roofed houses, three granaries, and a log cabin-style chicken coop raised off the ground on four poles. These structures looked like boards growing out of a boulder-strewn hill on which they had taken root.

On the opposite bank and a little farther downstream was another house and granary. It was on the valley floor, surrounded by fields of corn and beans and grassy areas where goats and sheep were grazing.

At the nearest household, boards had been laid over the top of a corn-drying platform, and piles of black and white wool had been set on the boards to dry in the sun. On a tree trunk leaning against a granary wall under the overhanging eaves there were great balls of woolen yarn hanging from the spikes where branches had been chopped off. These "coat hanger" limbs are an integral part of every Tarahumara household.

A young woman sat next to a horizontal broad loom by one of the granaries, busily weaving the homespun yarn into a heavy blanket. She had already spun the wool, using a simple wooden spindle twirled with the help of a large, encircling wooden whorl.

The big loom was more or less parallel to the ground, the common practice throughout most of northwestern Mexico. The side supports were tree trunks whose ends away from the weaver were held off the ground a few inches. The ends nearest where she sat merely rested on the ground. The loom's lower crosspiece was held in place by wedges or pegs driven into the side supports near the weaver. Forks in the trunks secured the upper crosspiece. The warp threads were continuously wrapped into a ring or tube over the two crosspieces. As the weaving advanced, the working point was kept at the same place by sliding the warp around the crosspieces. Blankets, sashes, and an occasional skirt are woven on such tubular rigs. The loom was completed by the addition of two shed rods and a heddle, devices which facilitate the over-and-under process of weaving. The weaver, who remained seated in one position at the end, worked in the weft threads using about three shuttles on each side. The shuttles held the woolen yarn just as a needle holds thread.

Most Tarahumara yarns are undyed natural wool, meaning the colors are predominantly black or white. For splashes of color and design, weavers buy or trade for commercially spun and dyed yarns or, more rarely today, they use indigo or other native dyes to color white yarns.

Finished blankets are loosely woven with coarsely spun yarns. This is no accident. The air spaces created add to the insulating quality of the blanket. Finely spun, tightly woven pieces may make good rugs, but the Tarahumaras are not interested in rugs. They are interested in protection against the sometimes bitter cold of the sierras. Nothing serves so well as a heavy, all-wool blanket.

Although it was pleasantly warm as we stood here and watched this patient woman work at her task, January experiences in these mountains have proven how cold it can become. Writing in the early eighteenth century, Father Fernández de Abee asserted, "The cold is so severe that the toes of the Indians fall off. This is seen in many of them." And Father Joseph de Escalona, writing at the same time from his mission at Sisoguichic, said, "The climate in this mission and its pueblos is so cold that many animals perish in the winter when they find no shelter. Bodies of Indians, frozen to death, are found in the

*Tarahumara* 57

*Weaving a woolen skirt*

*Spinning the yarn*

snow. They go out fearlessly to hunt deer and other animals that become torpid in the snow and are therefore easily caught.''

Those people found frozen in the snow were probably unfortunates on the way home from a tesgüinada, and they must have been without their blankets.

Inside one of the houses we could see preparations being made for supper. The principal chore for the women is to grind corn on a stone basin, called a *metate* in Spanish, with a handstone called a *mano*. The end product can be any one of five major corn dishes: pinole, esquiate, atole, tortillas, or tamales.

∽∾

If tesgüino is the Tarahumara national beverage, then *pinole* is their national food. It is prepared from shelled corn that has been removed from the cob by rubbing the cobs together. The kernels are put into a pottery vessel designed especially for the purpose. A handful of sand is thrown in with the kernels to assure even distribution of heat, and the pot is put on the fire to roast its contents. The corn is stirred constantly to keep it from burning. When the grains burst the contents are either put into a guari basket through which the sand can be sifted, or a spoon or sardine can on a stick is used to lift the roasted grains from the container.

The roasted corn is ground twice on a metate, the second grinding reducing the corn to a coarse flour. This corn meal is the pinole. It can be eaten as is, simply by using one's fingers to put the pinole in the mouth. More commonly, it is mixed with water or milk and drunk. Milk is rarely used, since Tarahumaras typically milk neither their cows nor their goats. In almost every household visited we were offered pinole in a half gourd. It has a very pleasant taste and, because the corn meal does not dissolve in water, it is slightly chewy.

*Esquiate*, on the other hand, is very much like American cornmeal mush. As in the preparation of pinole, corn is roasted in a roasting pot and the kernels are then ground twice on a metate. The difference is that with the second grinding a small amount of water is added to form a paste that is mixed with water and consumed at once.

*Atole* is cooked gruel made from corn that has been boiled several hours. Once it has been boiled, the corn is drained and mashed on the metate to form a thick paste. Water is added to the paste and the mixture is cooked by boiling. Atole can be eaten either while it is still hot or after it has been allowed to cool.

Tortillas, as already mentioned, are made from corn that has been boiled in water either with lime or oak ashes. The boiled corn is removed from the olla with a wooden spoon or gourd and washed with several changes of water. The end product is *nixtamal* which is twice ground on a metate. The resulting dough is shaped into balls and patted into round tortilla shapes. The tortillas are cooked on a flat pottery griddle called a *comal* in Spanish.

Tarahumaras make plain tamales, bean tamales, meat tamales, and green corn tamales. The first three are wrapped in corn husks and cooked in an olla. Meat tamales, which may include lizard meat, are the only ones with their ends tied. Green corn tamales are roasted rather than cooked in a pot.

*The corn grinder*

*Kitchen wall*

All these corn foods can be prepared with various additives, chili chief among them. Salt and lard can be added to the tamale batter. Beyond that, the roasted, crushed, or cooked parts of several other plants can be added as condiments to give different flavors to these otherwise very ordinary dishes.

Squash can be baked, boiled, ground, or dried; beans can be roasted and ground and made into a pinole-like dish or they can be soaked and boiled. Tarahumaras like their cooked beans a little on the chewy side.

Not very much is eaten in a wholly raw, uncooked, or undried state. Chicken eggs are occasionally sucked raw, as we saw for ourselves, and fruits are eaten without any special preparation. But fire enters into most food preparation. There is always a fire burning when people are at home. In former times fires were started with flint and steel strike-a-lights, and before that with a bow drill. Today virtually everyone has matches.

Before leaving this household, one of the day's mysteries was solved. Next to a granary were three more circular stones, turtleback in shape with flakes struck off the circumference. They were identical to the one found along the trail. Tarahumaras make them to use in a game of Indian-style quoits. The game is called *cuatro* in Spanish or *dihibápa* in Tarahumara. Lumholtz described this game as he saw it played in the 1890s:

> There is also a game very similar to quoits, played with stone disks, flat on one side and convex on the other. . . . Two and two play against each other. First one stone is moistened with spittle on one side to make it "heads or tails" and tossed up. The player who wins the toss plays first. Each has three stones, which are thrown toward a hole in the ground, perhaps twenty yards off. One of each party throws first, then goes to the hole and looks at it, while the other players make their throws. The stone falling nearest to the hole counts one point; if it falls into the hole, it counts four; if the stone of a second player falls on top of the first stone in the hole, it "kills" the first stone. The game is out at twelve. To measure distances, they break off small sticks. Lookers-on may stand around and bet which of the players will win.

On one occasion, when we tried to bring one of these gaming stones back to the Arizona State Museum, it was confiscated by Mexican border officials who insisted that such an object must be prehistoric. Little did they know, or believe, that people who lived fewer than 200 miles from where they were standing were still making these stone disks.

We left the women cooking and weaving and continued down the valley another half mile or so to the mouth of the stream. Here it emptied into a river and near the junction were three more households. One was a cave dwelling.

It was getting late, so we forded the river barefooted to reach an abandoned stone house standing on a bluff. The walls were simply piled rocks; at least a fourth of the

*Summer flowers and a pueblo church*

64   Tarahumara

*Engravers' art*

boards and canoes that once had been part of the roof were gone. Our tarps and plastic sheets were spread over the top and weighted down with rocks.

The wooden door to the structure, hinged to the threshold and lintel with wooden pintles, had been left ajar; goats and sheep had made this place a resting stop. But we were very tired, and dried goat and sheep manure made a comfortable mattress beneath our sleepnig bags.

By morning the river had dropped more than a foot since the evening before. We realized suddenly the opposite could happen. Given a really heavy rain we could have found ourselves stranded on the "wrong" side of the river, away from the households we hoped to visit during the next few days. This involved a hurried move to another abandoned stone house on the opposite side. Only this one had a solid rock floor. Dried manure is much softer.

The ranchos in the immediate vicinity had no church, but the people who lived here felt themselves, ceremonially and politically, to be a part of a pueblo six miles downriver which did, indeed, have a church.

Some pueblo churches are situated in settlements that were "Christianized" by the Jesuits in the seventeenth and eighteenth centuries, or by the Franciscans who followed them after 1767. Many of the church buildings themselves were erected in the eighteenth century on or near sites of still earlier structures. Many more churches were built in the nineteenth century, and still more have been constructed in the present century. They are in various states of repair and disrepair. Churches with resident priests or with priests living nearby are likely to be in better condition than those which see a priest only occasionally.

Churches dominate the landscape wherever they are. Always the biggest building in the pueblo, many have an atrium enclosed by a stone wall. Floor plans are rectangular, a nave and sanctuary without crossing and transepts. Usually a building is attached at one side, the *convento*, that serves as a sacristy and priest's quarters.

The interiors of pueblo churches range from being altogether plain to being elaborately decorated, some of them with wonderful folk designs applied by the local people. On a few there are carvings on the faces of building stones, graffiti, if you like. Some of these carvings, especially those of horses, have rare grace and charm.

Many churches have dirt floors; others have wooden floors; and still others have floors of stone. Handsome ceilings are common, including decorated axe-hewn vigas or beams supported on elaborately carved corbels on the walls.

Wherever churches are, with few exceptions, and especially if there are no clergy in residence, the buildings stand isolated and apart. If there were once Tarahumara houses near them, these have been moved away. If once proud and well kept, they show signs of weakening. Missions, wherever they stand, have become an integral part of the life of Tarahumaras, but only on Tarahumara terms. They are no more or less to the people than other man-made objects in the total environment, and are treated accordingly. In those places where the only church is falling totally into ruin, it signals that the tenuous Catholicism and Christianity of the Tarahumaras is doing likewise. The people have refused to be imposed upon, even if they have been hospitable and polite.

A cave dwelling was next on the agenda. In retrospect, it sounds foolish to mention it. "Cave dwellers!" It has such an exotic ring to our urban ears. But in the Sierra Tarahumara, there is nothing exotic about it. It suits the tenor of Tarahumara life so well that climbing the narrow foot trail chopped out of the rocks below the cave gave us a great sense of fit. Nothing, somehow, could be more natural or more sensible. A well-situated cave makes a fine dwelling place.

The people who lived here were absolutely no different than Tarahumaras who live in log cabins or in wooden lean-tos. In fact, one of the local women who now occupied a wooden house, was born in this very cave—and she was as civil and as "civilized" as anyone else. The cave was now home for an old woman, her son and daughter-in-law, and her two granddaughters. It came complete with a kitchen–sleeping area improved upon slightly by the addition of a rock wall; a wooden granary and a stone granary; a rock shelter used to store baskets, clothing, yard goods, and other potentially perishable items; a second rock shelter where goats and sheep were penned up for the night; and a

*Tarahumara* 67

*Native art in a decaying church interior*

*A falling monument to Christianity*

Tarahumara   69

*The place of caves and spires*

cliff-side boulder whose upslope base provided a nice place for the chickens to stay out of harm's way. Trash was disposed of easily. It was just tossed down the side of the cliff below.

It was a good climb down to the river, the nearest source of drinking and cooling water, and up again, so here and there near the mouth of the cave, people had hollowed out places in the rock that served as temporary catchment basins for rain water. These were also handy drinking bowls for chickens, dogs, and livestock.

Around the corner from the cave was another rock shelter, one large enough to accommodate a blanket loom and suitable for storing potter's clay and other materials.

The view, of course, was magnificent! One could see for miles, both upriver and downriver as well as across to the mountains on the opposite bank. And one could hear well too. The roof of the cave caught all the sounds immediately below, like a large echo chamber. As a Tarahumara man climbed up the trail to the cave, whistling a happy tune, as Tarahumaras are given to doing, he could be heard long before he was in clear sight at the cave's mouth.

In this country of volcanic tuff, caves or rock shelters come in clusters. Many caves formerly used as dwellings have been abandoned, either given over as animal corrals or given up entirely. Someday they will probably be occupied again. In smaller caves there are remains of the dead, one Tarahumara custom being to dispose of the bodies of the dead in sealed-off rock shelters. Within sight of the cave we were visiting was the cave crypt of the body of the husband of the elderly widow who lived here.

Not all Tarahumaras are buried in caves. Around pueblos there are usually church cemeteries; many people are inhumed beneath the earth. In either case, Tarahumaras have a healthy respect for the dead—they want as little as possible to do with burial caves or cemeteries. The belief is that the dead may want to harm the survivors, because they are lonely and would like to have the company of their relatives.

Not that burial caves are entirely sacrosanct. The most important of all Tarahumara sports are cross country kickball races run by the men. Tremendous stakes are often bet on the outcome. To get the edge in a race, sometimes one side will retrieve leg bones from a burial cave, grind them on a metate, and mix the powdered bone with the dirt of the race track. When the unsuspecting opponent runs over the contaminated spot, the dead grab his feet and cause him to lose.

When a person dies, his hands are tied together over his chest with a small cross in them and his body is wrapped in a blanket. A fire is built at his side. An additional small cross, draped with a rosary, is placed near the body. The person's possessions—food, clothes, axe, knife, violin, etc.—are put near the cross. Usually the body lies in state in the person's house; to get around the need to abandon the house later, the body may be placed in a shack or lean-to that is more expendable.

The deceased is the concern only of the immediate family. If they can, they take care of all the arrangements prior to burial, which takes place after the body has lain in state for one night. If it is a non-Christian burial, the family and possibly some helpers kneel

*Home in a cave*

*A cave closet*

by the corpse and speak to it in turn. They tell him he is dead and that he is being given plenty of food to take him safely into the next world. Moreover, they assure him that three fiestas will be given in his honor during the year (four if the deceased is a woman). They ask him to leave family members and friends in peace; to leave his possessions for those who are his rightful heirs; not to return to damage the crops or livestock.

Next a pole is cut and the corpse and blanket are fastened to it in the manner of a litter. Someone plays a violin tune and esquiate is sprinkled over the blanketed corpse. Two men carry the body to a burial cave while two men follow carrying the rosary and cross, the man's hat, and food. When they reach the cave, the entrance is uncovered; the body is pushed inside, but without the pole. The food, rosary, cross, and hat are pushed in after him, and the mouth of the cave is again closed off with rocks and mud.

When the pallbearers return, they undergo a brief and simple purification rite. Afterwards, the fire in the man's house is covered with juniper branches. All the family members and helpers undergo ceremonial cleansing by having themselves, their clothes, and the remaining clothes of the deceased thoroughly smoked. Then they eat pinole and ground chili in water. The men who assisted refrain from doing any work until the conclusion of the ensuing three-day fiesta lest the fields become sterile and the livestock sick.

Christian customs are much the same, except that the corpse is carried into the church where a candle is lighted by the body's head. A Tarahumara *maestro* recites Catholic prayers and sings Catholic songs. The maestro also gives a short sermon of counsel to the deceased.

The body is then carried to the cemetery where a deep grave has been dug. The blanketed corpse is lowered into the hole without the litter pole on which it has been carried; each worker puts a handful of dirt into the grave; men with shovels fill the hole and the top is covered with stones. Afterward the participants, their clothes, and their tools are given a ceremonial cleansing in the smoke of a juniper fire lighted in a nearby arroyo.

Three days after a man has died (four days for a woman) there has to be a small fiesta for the deceased. It is complete with the meat of a sacrificially killed goat or other animal, a dutubúri dance, and more food prepared and taken to the burial cave where the corpse has been placed.

Three weeks after the death of the man, a large fiesta is given. It includes the altar and three crosses erected at the edge of the dance patio, dutubúri dancing and chanting, goat meat, esquiate, and tesgüino. This fiesta also includes a rite to purify all of the dead man's possessions which have been left behind. If the deceased had been a runner, there might also be a ceremonial race held in his honor. If the deceased had been a woman who also had been a runner, the ceremonial race will involve men dressed as women. In some places, men wear women's clothing as a regular part of the observances at a woman's death fiesta.

At the conclusion of the three or four death fiestas it is hoped that the dead person has made a safe journey to heaven and the survivors' obligations have been met.

From community to community, there are variations on the funeral and death fiesta theme. In some places the fiestas are held over a three-year period; in others there is yúmari dancing in addition to the dutubúri.

Wendell Bennett tells us that among Tarahumaras death is not an occasion for great sadness. Death is accepted as a fact of life, and mourners are not given to overt expressions of grief. Except that she should not have relations with men nor remarry until her deceased husband is in heaven, there are almost no restrictions placed on widows. Fiestas, like Irish wakes, are times for enjoyment. Death is not considered an end but a change. The deceased has merely gone to the Land of the Dead, a land of opposites where night is the day of the dead and the moon is the source of heat and light.

The outstanding emotion of survivors is not grief, but fear. The dead are capable of all kinds of mischief. They can lure the living to join them; spoil tesgüino; kill cattle and sheep; spit and blow in the faces of people to make them ill; suffocate people; eat food that has been prepared for a feast. Because the dead are supposed to travel about at night, only shamans can travel safely after dark. Other Tarahumaras do not like to travel at night.

In spite of their own distaste for burial caves and human remains, Tarahumaras were apparently more than tolerant of Carl Lumholtz's 1890s archaeological activities. He reported:

> The Tarahumares had no great scruples about my removing the bodies of their dead, if the latter had died some years before and were supposed to have been properly dispatched from this world. Where a body had been buried, the bones that were not taken away had to be covered up again. One Tarahumare sold me the skeleton of his mother-in-law for one dollar.

Aside from supernatural concerns, death also occasions social problems for Tarahumaras. They believe in the private ownership of property, land as well as personal possessions, and inheritance is an important matter among them. Disputes over inheritance are among the most crucial to be considered by Tarahumara governors.

The ownership of a piece of agricultural land is customarily contingent upon its owner's keeping it in continual use. Six years is about as long as a piece of farm land can be kept idle before others may claim it. In this sense, then, "land rights" rather than "land ownership" may better describe the Tarahumara concept.

Anyone can clear and fence unused land for his own use, but this is largely academic because virtually all land in the Sierra Tarahumara that can be farmed is already claimed. This means that the remaining ways to acquire land rights are through trade, sale, or inheritance, the latter being the most common means. People recognize that their livelihood depends on having rights to land; there is strong resistance to selling it or trading it. But when one who owns such rights dies, that person's heirs will inherit them.

Men and women are equal in their rights to land. When one or the other dies, their children are supposed to inherit equally. That is to say, all children have equal rights to all of the property—land and otherwise—of the deceased parent. If there are no children, then siblings are next in succession. They are followed by grandchildren.

Tarahumaras believe that each adult should have enough land to provide for his or her needs. The inheritance system strives toward that kind of distribution.

*Pottery still life*

76   Tarahumara

*Polishing a pot*

*Working on a second vessel*

78   Tarahumara

There can be also advance inheritance, in which a child is allowed to take over his share of the inheritance when he marries. Access to land can further be obtained through marriage when a man moves away to marry a woman in some distant rancho who has land rights of her own. The man works his wife's land and they share its products.

Grazing land is open range free to be used by anyone.

Visiting the people living in the cave and looking around at the furnishings reminded us of the close relationship between the people and their surroundings. About ninety percent of the household furnishings were made by Tarahumaras themselves out of materials more or less readily at hand. All that was required to acquire them was human energy; all that was needed to make them was knowledge of tradition and skill. One of the ladies, learning of our interest in such things, invited us to her house where she planned to make some pots. Her invitation was accepted, and early one morning we walked up a little side stream to a lovely meadow where her house, granary, and corral were located and where she was living with two daughters and a niece. Her husband and son were away working as laborers in a Mexican sawmill for $50.00 peso per day (a little more than $2.00 per day).

As soon as we had arrived she hurried up to a flat rock on the hill behind her house where there was a large can filled with dried and finely ground clay. It was clay gathered from a favorite deposit more than six miles away. She had ground it on a metate and mixed it with pottery sherds that had also been ground on a metate. These ground sherds provided the temper.

Pouring the clay onto the rock into a slight depression, she added water to it from a bucket brought from her house. She kneaded the water and clay together, rolling and folding and pounding it as if preparing bread dough. More water and more clay were added from time to time.

In less than twenty minutes she had a large lump of thoroughly dampened clay the consistency of soft leather. She picked it up and carried it back down the hill to her house to the kitchen–sleeping area where the clay would be shaped into vessels.

Tearing off a lump of the clay dough, she sat on the ground next to a guari basket that had a piece of cloth over it and proceeded to model the base of the clay pot by hand. When the small bowl base had taken shape, walls of the new vessel were built by adding ropes or coils of clay to the rim in succeeding layers until it had reached the desired height. All the time she kept her hands moist and kept smoothing and thinning the walls by hand and with the help of a piece of gourd used as a scraper-smoother. Everything, including the final rim of the vessel, was modeled by hand and gourd scraper.

Working in a steady rhythm without pausing, she always knew exactly what to do next. She turned the vessel simply by turning the basket and cloth on which it rested. Her thumb and fingers found their way inside the growing vessel to smooth out the places where the coils had been attached to the rim. She tore more clay from the ball of dough as she needed it. The vessel took shape and came to life before our very eyes, a

*A potter's cache*

80   Tarahumara

genuine miracle of creation. Her first vessel, after drying in the sun and after being fired in a shallow pit with a very hot fire, would be a bean pot.

She continued, making two more pots, each one with a different shape and each with a different intended use. They would be baked to a brittle hardness in a day or two, after we had gone. Most likely they would not be painted. Their art was in their form rather than in their surface decoration. Plainware pottery is the Tarahumara rule, altogether in keeping with their straightforward way of life. Much of the essence of Tarahumara life is captured in their pottery. It is functional; it is not complex; it is a product of the immediate interaction between people and their close surroundings. There are pottery bowls from which to eat; tesgüino cooking vessels and tesgüino fermenting jars; roasting pots; *comales* for frying things; pots for boiling beans, corn, and greens.

Some pottery, of course, is decorated. As more of it makes its way into the commercial market, inevitably more of it will be decorated. Our potter pointed to a simple design on an old pot in her kitchen and explained to us that her husband had used his fingers to paint it.

If pottery is inorganic, and I am not altogether sure that is the right way to think of it, then basketry is most certainly organic. Nearly every Tarahumara woman, and many of the men, knows how to make baskets using the leaves of beargrass or of palm trees (found in the barrancas). Some basket makers even use pine needles.

On all our trips into the Sierra Tarahumara we have seen basket makers at work. It is something that can be done when one is sitting down to tend the flocks. It can be done at home in between other chores, the materials set aside to be picked up again when it is convenient.

Like Tarahumara pottery, their basketry is the essence of simplicity. There are no decorations woven in; the beauty lies in the form and in the sense of utility conveyed.

All Tarahumara baskets are plaited. Both the lidless guari basket and the lid-covered *petacas*, like the *petate* (a mat), are twill plaited. Most are single weave, but in the barrancas and in parts of eastern Tarahumara country baskets are made in a double weave, especially the petacas.

The only tools needed by a basket maker are her hands and teeth. However, to keep from getting cut on the sharp edges of the beargrass, she will probably first run the U-shaped leaves between her thumb and a soft stone, the edges against the stone. These stones develop deep grooves, objects that may one day tantalize archaeologists trying to decipher their purpose.

Baskets are used for all kinds of things. For a people who quite literally live on the ground, baskets are the means of keeping objects out of the dirt and segregated from one another. Taking the place of cabinets, cupboards, and drawers, they are filled with corn, seeds, herbs, sewing material, weaving material, condiments, safety pins, matches, utensils, and just about everything imaginable. In one household we were startled one evening to see a guari basket that had been tipped upside down moving across the floor. It was being powered by baby chicks that had been put there for the night to make sure the family cat would not eat them. It was a moving basket with peeping sound effects.

Although baskets are light, they are bulky. To make them easier to store or to carry, basket makers shape guaris in graduated sizes. This way they can be nested together. Some nests of baskets have as many as forty individual pieces.

Late one afternoon as we walked along a trail by the side of the river, we saw a man standing on a rock at the water's edge holding a long spear. He was fishing, poking the pointed nose of the spear into an area of still water beneath a submerged boulder. Did he really think he was going to catch anything? Or was this, as fishing so often is with us, a form of quiet recreation?

Should he spear some fish, they would be taken home, filleted, strung on a wire to dry and later tossed on a fire for a quick roasting before being eaten, heads, tails and all.

Should he get no fish, what would it matter? He could whistle on his way home and, when he got there, get out his homemade violin and play a few tunes for his own enjoyment and for that of his family. This life requires work, the expenditure of energy; but it also provides serenity, dignity, and a wholeness that has become alien to our urban way of living.

Our visits with Tarahumaras suggested that they have great respect for themselves and for the rights of other individuals. They are shy and generally quiet, but ready with a smile or laugh. They are self-reliant in their mountain surroundings, able to take from the environment their most basic and essential foods and tools.

They have invested heavily in one another: in the household, in the rancho or pueblo community, and in the circle of people on whom they can call for help and with

*Cornelio's father*

whom they can share corn beer. Such investments work against the accumulation of material wealth, because they cannot prosper in the face of acquisitiveness. So a Tarahumara's wealth is primarily in himself and in the numbers of family members and friends upon whom he can rely for help and companionship. To those of us who live in a world in which the primacy of the family and household has been in a state of siege, the sense of unity, warmth, and affection projected by a Tarahumara family—whether living in a cave or cabin—is astounding. It is also reassuring. Here in the mountains, at least, a very old-fashioned form of love has survived.

84   Tarahumara

# CHAPTER FIVE

The Christmas music was supplied by a piano. When I talk about a piano at Batopilas after you have read of the travel it took to reach this place [deep at the bottom in the barranca country], naturally you are entitled to know how its possession was possible. There were no balloons, and if there had been, they never could have dropped down into that steep-sided canyon which was five thousand feet deep. There were no airplanes and no place to land even if there had been such means of transportation. From what you have read you will realize that although a pack-mule with his arriero [muleteer] is capable of carrying almost unthinkable loads, you cannot see him coming along the mountain trails with an upright piano draped across his back.

But don't forget that we still have the Indian.

If you have the time to spare and if you have a clever Mexican who understands the Indian and who speaks his language, and if you leave it to them with no suggestions on your part, that cumbersome box will eventually arrive, and arrive right side up. It is really quite simple.

When it is unloaded from the wagon at Carichic [in the northern part of the Sierra Tarahumara] you cut two long straight pine poles. It is better to have them already cut and the bark removed so that they will be dry and properly seasoned. They ought to be about four inches in diameter at the big end. Put one on either side of the piano in its wooden box and tie them in such a way that the weight is balanced with no tendency to be top-heavy when lifted from the ground. I suggest that you allow the Mexican to do the tying of the ropes; they make a very good job of such things. You now have a piano in a box with two poles the ends of which stick out far enough to have plenty of room for at least two Indians to get under the end of each pole; this makes four of them at

85

*each end of the piano. They get under the poles in a squatting position;*
*at the word "Vamanos!" they straighten up. The piano is off the ground,*
*and the carriers move off with inward satisfaction of knowing that all*
*they have to do now is carry this great box for a hundred and eighty-five*
*miles in fifteen or twenty days. There will be at least twenty-four car-*
*riers—that makes three sets—and they spell each other every twenty or*
*thirty minutes. They are well fed at your expense if you want a maxi-*
*mum of efficiency. Each man is paid at the rate of a dollar a day. At the*
*end of the journey he takes his "easy money" and trots back home a*
*hundred and eighty miles or more in about three days, and he has a*
*happy time for some months on his ill-gotten gains!*

GRANT SHEPHERD
*The Silver Magnet*, 1938

THEY CALL THEMSELVES the *Rarámuri*, "footrunners." We wanted to see for ourselves, so we arranged a race between two pairs of girls. One pair of girls, older than the other, lived near a Mexican settlement and their lives were fairly sedentary. The second pair lived in one of the remote ranchos we were visiting. The outcome was preordained, but we went ahead anyway, one hundred pesos to each of the winners and fifty pesos to each of the losers. It seemed like a good investment of some thirteen or fourteen dollars.

Before the race could begin, the racing tools had to be made. These were four branches carved smoothly into slightly curved sticks about three feet long and two hoops about seven inches in diameter made from beargrass. Each girl was given one stick; each team was given one hoop. The race is called *dowérami*, the *dowéra* being the curved stick.

A short course was laid out along the river's edge where the girls were to run over existing trails. The trails moved up and down, in some places over rocks. One of us stood about a half-mile from the starting point to serve as the turnaround marker. The race was to be over when the girls had run three complete circuits, or about three miles. They were too polite to tell us that such a short race is silly.

The race began, and the four girls dashed along using their sticks to throw the hoop ahead of them. They were supposed to take turns lifting the hoop only with their sticks and tossing it ahead of them again, but in this race the first team member to reach the hoop picked it up, even if she was the person who had thrown it. Sometimes they ran for several yards carrying the hoop on the stick before they threw it again. But we were not there to judge.

Before the first half lap was run the "city" girls dropped far behind. However, they never stopped and no one showed any sign of lagging on purpose. Once in a while the girls smiled as they ran past us, but generally their minds were on the business of running. Three were barefooted; one wore sandals. All were breathing heavily. And why shouldn't they have been—at approximately 7,000 feet above sea level and running with all their might?

The race seemed to be over almost before it began. We were too busy taking pictures to clock it, but certainly their time was excellent. The local, "country" girls won handily, almost a half-mile ahead of the other team. Within less than a minute after the race had ended, all four girls sat on the grass at the finishing point and smiled shyly as they received their reward money. They were no longer breathing heavily and, in fact, gave no indication of any kind that they had just run three miles. A real race, after all, would have gone on for many miles and for many hours, sometimes all night.

While women are good racers, they are not as good as the men. The men are famous throughout the region for the kickball race, the *rarahipa*. Tarahumaras are famous for gambling on the outcome of the races. "The betting," says Wendell Bennett, "is intense."

The course of each race is decided on just before the race starts. The "track," which is likely to include streams, gullies, rocky slopes, fences, meadows, and brush-strewn hillsides, is normally anywhere from two to twelve miles long. The number of required laps depends on how long the race is supposed to last. A short race will require only a few hours; a long race will take a day and a night or longer. A count is kept of the number of laps by setting a row of stones at the starting point and removing one stone each time a lap is completed.

The race pits one team against another, each side having from two to a dozen runners. The object is to get a team's wooden ball, about four inches in diameter, over the finish line first. While a ball can be put back on the course by using one's hands, it cannot be propelled forward in any way other than by kicking it or, actually, tossing it with the foot. The racers are barefooted. When one of them comes up to the ball, he stops, gets his toes under it, and tosses it ahead with a mighty kick. His teammates are farther down the track waiting to receive the ball. The race progresses in relay fashion.

Runners can drop out temporarily to drink pinole, be tended by a shaman, or answer nature's call, but they cannot kick the ball again until they have run as many laps as the ball has advanced. Spectators line the route to cheer their team and watch for possible fouls; watchers are waiting at the end-markers to see that turns are properly made; in large races, the governor and a couple of appointed judges referee complaints. Fouls include pushing, shoving, fighting, tripping, and, most dastardly of all, pulling off the loincloth of an opponent.

Three nights before a big race the runners make fairly elaborate preparations. They rub their legs with goat grease or olive oil and with boiled juniper branches. The night before the race they seclude themselves as a team with four elderly men, some of whom may be shamans. Each runner, in turn, holds the team's kickball and his own stick while his legs are washed in a boiled juniper solution by one of the elders. He makes three turns where he stands, hands the stick and ball to one of the old men, takes a drink of laurel, and goes to sleep. The kickball is painted white or marked with a blue or red cross to distinguish it. The stick is the one each contestant is allowed to carry to dislodge the ball from difficult places.

If the runners are hungry the night before the race, they eat tortillas, esquiate, and beans and drink coffee or warm water. They may also smoke strong cigarettes. Old men in attendance drink tesgüino if they choose, but not the men who are to race.

Some Tarahumara runners wear rattling belts as they race. Strings of deer hoofs, reeds, or metallic cartridges are attached to leather belts. Their rattling is supposed to keep the runners awake.

After nightfall the way is lighted either by resinous pine torches or, more commonly, by tin lanterns carried on the ends of poles and in which pine pitch is burned. These, and now flashlights as well, are carried by the spectators.

"Betting," as Wendell Bennett points out, "is one of the most important parts of the race." He goes on to explain:

> An Indian will wager almost anything he possesses. Knives, beads, cloth, blankets, cows, wool, and even land, may be bet. The runners themselves are among the heaviest betters and thus run in earnest. If the runners do not place bets, the people are afraid, and they too refrain from betting. The economic aspect of the races increases the interest in them.
>
> Each team has from one to four [directors], who collect all the bets and deal with the [directors] of the other side. The bets are carefully matched. Cloth is measured piece by piece, beads are matched, and animals are carefully compared. All bets are tied together in bundles and deposited in one place. Even cows are tied together. If the bet is not tangible, it must be settled within a few days. The night after the race, when the big celebration fiesta is in progress, a large fire is built near the bets. The [director] from the winning team holds up a bundle and shouts, "Whose is this?" The owner (winner) comes forward and claims his bundle, which contains both his original bet and his winnings.

Lumholtz says a man will bet everything he has in this world except his wife and children. "He draws the line at that." And he scrupulously pays all his gambling debts.

Big races between two communities invariably include a full-scale tesgüinada. Bennett has observed that the general intermingling that goes on at these races and at the tesgüinada assists people from different communities to become better acquainted, and that the competition of the race helps solidify community members into units of *we* and *they*. It is also clear that such races and the attendant betting serve still another function: wealth is distributed throughout the total region and is less likely to be accumulated by any one person or community. Given the scarcity of land, food, and material goods in the Sierra Tarahumara, such a system enables the goods that are available to go further. Although some runners are obviously more skilled than others, all Tarahumaras recognize the element of chance in the races. Moreover, they believe strongly that the supernatural influences the final outcome. According to Lumholtz, "A race is never won by natural means. The losers always say that they have been bewitched by the others."

Tarahumaras, both men and women, can be said to start training for races as soon as they are old enough to walk. Because as soon as they learn to walk, they begin to run. Living in a country that is as much up and down as it is flat and where the most practical means of transportation is by foot does a lot to get one in condition in a very short time. Sedentary city dwellers that we are, even we noticed that after a few days in Tarahumara back country distances began to seem shorter, hills less steep, and water closer at hand.

*Runners on the trail*

To people who have lived here all their lives, it must seem that all their country is flat and that everyplace is close to everyplace else.

The high protein, low meat, vitamin-enriched diet of the Tarahumaras—when they can get enough of their own food—in combination with the natural conditioning of their whole way of life, makes them superb endurance runners and objects of curiosity to western medical practitioners. It is true there is a high infant mortality rate, but this is due largely to infant diarrhea and untreated diseases to which infants are susceptible. It is also true that the life expectancy of Tarahumaras is about forty-five years of age. Their lives are shortened by bronchial disorders, colds, fevers, rheumatism, sores, wounds, and gastrointestinal disorders induced at least partially by the total lack of sanitary facilities. There are no toilet facilities of any kind; Tarahumaras do not use toilet paper or any substitute for it. And with so many cattle, sheep, and goats grazing near the streams and springs, it is not surprising that much of the drinking water is contaminated.

The problem with their diet is that Tarahumaras often do not get enough to eat. If the rains have not been abundant, malnutrition and even starvation can prevail.

Illness aside, their extraordinary physical condition cannot be denied. Frederick Schwatka, who was in the Sierra Tarahumara ahead of Lumholtz, told of a Tarahumara who carried mail from Chihuahua City to mining camps in the foothills of the Sierra Madre. This man "made the round trip with his thirty or forty pounds of mail and provisions in just six days, resting Sundays in Chihuahua to see the bullfight. This distance is over 500 miles, half of it being on as rough and hazardous a mountain trail as any in the known world." He also told about an Indian who carried a message from the rim above the Barranca del Cobre to the bottom of the canyon some 4,000 or 5,000 feet below and returned to the top in an hour and twenty minutes.

Lumholtz pointed out that Tarahumaras are not great sprinters and are not particularly fast. Rather, they run steadily, hour after hour, mile after mile. Lumholtz said a good runner could make forty miles in six or eight hours. He once clocked a race in which the runners, kicking a ball ahead of them, covered twenty-one miles in two hours. The lead man ran 290 feet in nineteen seconds on the first lap and the next in twenty-four seconds. He also recalled a Tarahumara who took five days to carry a letter from Guazapares to Chihuahua City and return, a distance of nearly 600 miles. Indians in the 1890s were hired by Mexicans to run wild horses into the corral, the same way they habitually ran down deer.

The reputation of Tarahumaras as endurance runners spread far beyond the boundaries of the Sierra Tarahumara. In 1926 two racers were invited to Mexico City to show what they could do. The New York *World* newspaper told the story:

> *Skeptics, who had received with a grain of salt the amazing stories of Tarahumara Indians running for days and nights unceasingly in their native Chihuahua wilds, were prepared to believe almost anything when they saw the two Indians to-day run without signs of fatigue a distance that would exhaust most horses, and doing this at an altitude of from a mile and a half to two miles, where many persons find breathing difficult even after slight exertion.*

*Matriarch*

*Zafiro and San Miguel started this morning at 3:05 at Pachuca bearing a letter from the Governor of Hidalgo State. All the way to Mexico City they kept up their pace. They continued across the city to the Athletic Stadium, and in the presence of a great cheering crowd delivered the letter to Governor Serrano of the Federal District, who was surrounded by a party of high government officials.*

*Instead of the laurel wreath bestowed upon the ancient Greek Marathon runners, Governor Serrano placed around the brow of each Indian a bright crimson silk bandanna handerchief—their favorite adornment. Throughout the race each had carried a red cotton one.*

*Mexico City sportsmen and government officials intend to petition the international sporting authorities to accept the Tarahumares' record as official, and also to include a 100-kilometer race in the program of the 1928 Olympic Games at Amsterdam, in which case Mexico will see that the Tarahumares are there.*

These two men covered sixty-five miles in nine hours and thirty-seven minutes. About a year later, two other Tarahumara runners ran from San Antonio to Austin, Texas, doing the 89.4 miles in fourteen hours and fifty-three minutes. There is also a story—this one probably apocryphal—that in the 1920s a Tarahumara governor was invited to send some runners to a marathon being held in Kansas. When the governor learned the distance was to be a mere 26 miles, he sent three girls to run it.

In more recent times, physiologists, physicians, and physical anthropologists have interested themselves in the Tarahumaras' extraordinary running ability. Studies were made of runners who ran a short kickball race of 28.6 miles. The average speed of the winning team was 5.81 miles per hour. Each contestant lost five pounds of weight during the contest; two of the runners had diastolic blood pressure readings of zero during and immediately at the end of the race, rising within a few minutes to 60 to 80. "Probably not since the days of the ancient Spartans," observed one of the doctors making the measurements, "has a people achieved such a high state of physical conditioning."

Tarahumara resting heart rates and blood pressure are about twenty percent below normal, although for Tarahumaras who have been living a sedentary life in mission centers or elsewhere, the rates and pressures are more like those of the population at large. Kickball racers can use more than 10,000 kilocalories per twenty-four hours, a level of consumption presumed to be at the outer limits of human work endurance. One twenty-eight-year-old man was found who was able to run continuously in hilly country over a period of four days and three nights without sleep. He could maintain an average speed of about 11.5 miles per hour for several hours at a stretch.

On one of our trips into the Sierra Tarahumara we visited the home of an elderly man and discovered he had an enormous tesgüino cooking pot in his house. Although it was cracked and a piece was gone from the rim, we decided to buy this thirty- to forty-gallon container. Its owner was more than happy to sell it to us, and he even repaired the crack in the side while we watched, using melted pine pitch daubed on the end of a stick. The problem, however, was how to get this huge earthenware vessel, which weighed at

*Village elder*

least fifty pounds, from his house at the bottom of a canyon to a mountain top where we had a truck parked. The distance was fully six miles by the shortest possible route over the face of a cliff; seven or eight miles by a longer route that avoided the cliff. And it was all uphill.

We asked the man, grey-haired and bent over from years of hard work, if he knew anyone who might be willing to carry the pot up to the truck for a hundred pesos (a little more than four dollars). He said, much to our surprise, that he would be glad to, but he would need a blanket or tarpaulin to carry it. We agreed that the next day he should come by our camp to get a blanket. We paid him and left.

When he had not arrived by noon the following day, we returned to his house to see what had happened. When we walked inside, he was there but the pot was gone! "Where's the pot?" we wanted to know.

"Oh," he answered, "I took that up there last night."

He had made a twelve- to sixteen-mile round trip in the pitch dark over a narrow footpath carrying this heavy and cumbersome tesgüino jar, just how we will never know. Moreover, he was as casual about it as if he had merely walked across a street to the grocery store to get a loaf of bread.

"How could that old man have done it?" I asked.

"Maybe," came the answer, "no one has ever told him he is old."

# CHAPTER SIX

*T*he church fiestas *would find no place in a study of the primitive (pre-Columbian) elements of Tarahumara culture. . . . It is not possible to assign an exact date to the introduction of these fiestas, but at least it has been within the last forty or fifty years that they have obtained a foothold. The priests taught them to the Indians but they have developed far beyond the extent of that original teaching. They have encroached upon and absorbed native elements, and have been amplified by native imagination until today they form one of the most important parts of the social structure of the Tarahumaras.*

WENDELL C. BENNETT
in *The Tarahumara*, 1935

EPIPHANY, from the Greek word for "manifestation," occurs on January 6 and it marks the end of the Christmas season. It is, in fact, the last day of Christmas, or Twelfth-day. With Easter and Pentecost, it is one of the three oldest festival days in the Christian church. It commemorates the manifestation of the Lord Jesus Christ to the Gentiles in the person of the Magi and is thus the Feast of the Three Holy Kings (*Pascua de Reyes* in Spanish). It also commemorates the manifestation of His divinity, as it occurred at His baptism in the Jordan River and when He performed His first miracle at Cana in Galilee when He turned water into wine at a wedding feast.

Tarahumaras celebrate Epiphany by turning corn into beer.

That, of course, is not their only Epiphany miracle. They also transform some of their number into tightly disciplined, precision dancers, their faces hidden with scarves and their heads covered by wooden-framed crêpe paper hats. Each dancer carries a wand in his left hand and a gourd rattle or Mexican *maraca* in the other. His shirt or blouse and

Mexican trousers are largely hidden by shawls and scarves around his neck and waist and over his back. He wears Mexican shoes rather than Indian sandals. He is a *matachine*.

Other ordinary people also undergo a change, transformed from Tarahumara citizen to Tarahumara fiddler or guitar player. Some of the fiddlers, especially, are virtuosi. With homemade bows and violins they can make one instrument sound like a string ensemble; with a dozen of them inside the nave of a church they produce as much sound as the whole string section of a major symphony orchestra. Their fast-paced rhythmic tunes, probably old Spanish airs played with a Tarahumara accent, may not please connoisseurs of classical music. But these musicians are fiddlers par excellence; they are not violinists. They play for hours on end, hypnotically, much to their enjoyment, if much to the ennui of others who fail to recognize the differences in the tunes and who characterize the music as "monotonous."

In short, Tarahumaras celebrate Epiphany, as they do the Feast of Guadalupe and Christmas, with a tesgüinada and matachine dancing to the accompaniment of fiddle and guitar music.

Matachine dancing occurs through Hispanic America and in regions where there has been considerable Hispanic influence. The Pueblo Indians of the Rio Grande in New Mexico, for example, have matachine dancers; so do the Yaqui Indians of Sonora and Arizona and a large number of mestizo communities throughout the Southwest and northern Mexico. I have even seen matachine dancers in the little town of Morgan Hill in northern California.

The origins of the dancing remain obscure. No doubt similar dances were performed in Spain and elsewhere in Europe as early as the fifteenth century, and there is even a possibility that matachine dancing is related to the ancient morris dance of England. What is confusing is that Spaniards coming into Mexico early in the 1500s found Aztecs performing similar dances. All one can suggest at the moment is that matachine dances are essentially European in origin and flavor, but that Indian elements, possibly including the gourd rattle, have crept into them. The violin and guitar which traditionally are played to accompany the dancing are altogether European, even if homemade by the natives.

Matachine dancing is usually performed by from eight to twelve brightly costumed men, although for major fiestas such as that of Epiphany, there may be as many as two dozen or more in the larger pueblos. The pièce de résistance of the matachine costume is the headdress. Called a crown or *corona* in Spanish, it consists of a wooden framework to which are attached colored paper or cloth ribbons, mirrors or mirror fragments, sequins, shiny buttons, or virtually anything to add glitter. The leader of the dance group is called the *monarco* (the "monarch"), and he may have a cross or some other distinguishing embellishment on his corona. Sometimes there are two monarcos in a group.

The wands carried by the dancers are usually in the shape of hearts on the end of wooden handles and are decorated with colored paper. The dancers carry Mexican manufactured maracas, gourd rattles, or rattles made by gluing wood shavings around a stick.

Each matachine dancer is under the charge of a *chapeón*. While the dance is in progress the *chapeónes* stand to one side marking time and shouting in falsetto voices. Al-

*Matachine musician*

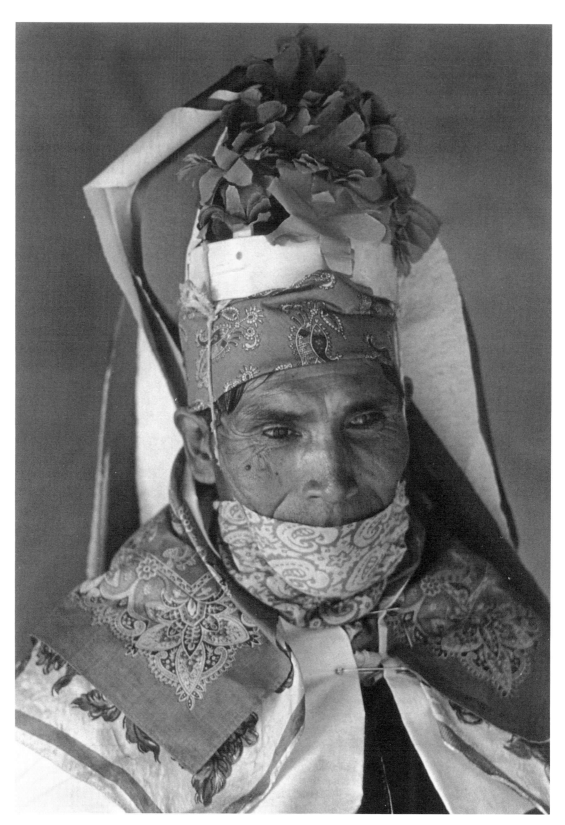

*El Monarco*

though each matachine makes his own costume, it is the job of the chapeón to see to it that his dancer's costume conforms in a general way to the others. One man is considered to be the head chapeón, and as such he is an important functionary. In some communities he wears as a symbol of his position a wooden carved mask. Some of these are painted and have false hair and beards glued to them. The head chapeón wears this mask on the back of his head while the dancing is in progress. Should he actually take part in the dancing, he joins the dancers at the end of the line and wears the mask over his face but does not shout. The chapeones also carry a special whip to keep the dogs away from the dancers. It is made from the inflated bladder of a bull and is attached to a handle made from a bull's penis.

Among the Mayo Indians of Sonora and Sinaloa, the whip bearers of the matachine group are called *chicatones* rather than chapeones, and the head of the chicatones is the *capitán*. Mayo matachines, like those of the Tarahumaras, also have monarcos.

Wendell Bennett has probably done the best job to date of describing the Tarahumara matachine dance. He points out that in general it is a fast-moving, twirling, shifting dance, performed by two columns of dancers under the direction of a leader. He continues:

> The dance resembles the Virginia reel vaguely. The dancers form a double column facing the musicians. The monarco, who stands in front, indicates all movements with the fan [wand] which he carries in his left hand. All dancers beat time with their rattles while dancing. After a few phrases of the music, the leader begins the dance by marking time and shaking his rattle. At a signal from him, all the dancers whirl around in their places, first to the left, then to the right. Next, the two lines cross over and change places. The left and right whirl is repeated, while the leader spins around between the columns. Then the lines cross back to their original places. Now the leader starts a grand right and left, alternating between lines. Every dancer turns when the monarco goes around him, until, at the end of the movements, all are facing away from the musicians. At this point, the movements are repeated until the original positions are assumed again, with the leader in front and the dancers facing the orchestra. Another movement follows in which the leader takes the head position of one column and leads it in a circular course around the other column. The other column tacks on at the end, and thus a circle is inscribed, ending with the dancers in their original positions. Now the movements are repeated, until, after about ten minutes, the dance is finished. However, the finish is only a breathing spell, because the dancers hold their places and after two or three minutes repeat the whole dance. The dancing is kept up for an hour or more (sometimes as long as three hours). Then there is a real rest, during which the formation breaks up and a general hubbub of smoking and chattering commences. The chapeones *stand in a line to one side of the dancers. They mark time during the dance and, at changes of movement, shout in falsetto voices.*

*A matachine*

*Matachine dancers*

I visited an Epiphany celebration at one of the larger churches in Tarahumara country in January, 1977. The celebration actually began on the eve of the last day of Christmas, or on the Twelfth-night. It started about 9:00 P.M inside the church when the matachines, chapeones, fiddlers, and spectators took up their respective positions. The women and children, as is customary, sat on the right side of the nave facing the altar; the men, including a row of eight fiddlers, sat to the left; the two dozen matachines and their fewer chapeones were in the center. A Jesuit priest officiated, and after making a greeting and a few announcements in the Tarahumara language, he sat down as the matachines put on their colorful headdresses, the fiddlers struck up a tune, and the dancing began in the church.

After a single dance lasting about ten minutes, all the dancers, musicians, and spectators formed into a crude column and began a procession which went out from the church into the freezing night air. It included a man carrying a processional cross surrounded by matachines and female acolytes reciting prayers and singing Christmas carols—such as Silent Night—in Spanish. Three wooden torches were lighted to add to the illumination of bonfires near the plaza in front of the church and of the nearly full moon which kept ducking behind clouds. Even as the women sang and prayed, the matachines danced and the fiddlers kept up their music. The chapeones barked their falsetto cries into the night. A Christmas tree with blinking colored lights stood in the window of a Mexican house near the plaza; the aroma of burning pinyon and juniper from warming fires descended on us.

The procession made a counter-clockwise circuit around the church, pausing five times: in front of the church, on its south, east, and north sides, and once again in front on the west. Everyone went back into the church; a Mass was celebrated, with the sermon being preached in Spanish and repeated in Tarahumara; matachine dancing took place until about 1:00 A.M. The dancing concluded and everyone left the church. The matachines and the rest of the Tarahumaras made their way out of the pueblo—which was largely inhabited by Mexicans—to a Tarahumara household on the outskirts of the village.

I went back to my room with a Mexican family to get some sleep, thinking the Tarahumaras would return to the church at 5:30 on Epiphany morning. I missed the tesgüinada. But in the early 1930s Robert Zingg watched a matachine dance held to celebrate Christmas, and he attended the tesgüinada. He didn't want to return to his room in the wing of the church, "with its bloodless celibatarian and ecclesiastical associations."

*So I edged into the last house and found sitting room among the Indians that jammed the place. I sat between two Tarahumara friends. Each would whisper confidentially to me at once. I would nod my head gravely, without, however, understanding a word uttered. Then I would whisper back at them, one at a time. They would gravely nod as I had done before. The scene was quite lively and animated. And I was a part of this primitive festivity. Indeed, I was so integrally a part of it that I could hardly crawl out of bed the next day. But that was a trifling forfeit.*

*The light of the roaring fire played throughout the room, revealing in bulking outline the forms of Indians in an interesting variety of postures. Here a wife watched over the recumbent body of her slumbering husband lest, in his drunken insensitivity, he might burn his feet in the fire. There a husband, his jealousy dulling the effects of the beer, crouched vigilantly beside his tipsy mate, as if afraid she might slip away from him in the hub-bub and join some waiting lover. At such brawls these little breaches of fidelity are not uncommon. I distinctly recall the hawklike visage of one old fellow who scrutinized me alertly for fear I might offer attentions to his wife. Finally he keeled over and fell into a drunken sleep.*

*Even more vividly do I remember the dark, flashing eyes of a Tarahumara girl, who gazed haughtily at me from the door. In the interracial language of the eyes of youth [Zingg was about 31 at the time] they said, "No, I am not for you." And they seemed to really mean it—though I had no intentions of leaving my snug corner by the fireplace anyway. I had never seen her before, nor did I see her after; so I cannot imagine why I was made the recipient of such a brilliant but haughty glance which for an instant sparkled like a fire-opal in the lurid atmosphere.*

*Others were still going strong. There was considerable laughter, for Tarahumaras surprisingly free and raucous. One woman got up and weaved through a slightly voluptuous dance for the special benefit of the violinist, for such men prove attractive figures to the belles of [this pueblo]. He, however, paid no attention. Finally she gave him what she thought was a gentle, lover-like shove. But her efforts were too vigorous; her push sent him over on his back, and there he remained.*

*Happy Tarahumara nights, the drink, the warmth, the congeniality, the close contact with the Indians, the bright roaring fire casting a weird light on the equally weird scene! These occasions always gave me such a feeling of contentment and oneness with the Indians, that for once in my anthropological career I felt I was seeing what everyone in my profession should see—the real spirit of the people under observation.*

I woke up at 5:30 in the morning. The pueblo, and the church, were quiet. It was obvious there was no Mass. So shortly before 7:00 I dressed and went to the front steps of the church, thinking that surely the matachines would soon return from where they had been celebrating. Someone's scavenging pig and I shared the plaza. The pig went away. A half hour later, still surrounded by silence, I went away too. There would be no Mass on this Twelfth-day. The Twelfth-night had taken its toll. The corn had been turned into beer and those at the feast had drunk it.

# CHAPTER SEVEN

*I*n retrospect, it is difficult to put into words my feelings during that first night in the pueblo. We had, after all, been flown in a very short space of time from the end of the seventh decade of the 20th century into the late 19th or very early 20th century; from an urban setting to a wholly rural setting; from a place where all things are known and familiar to a place where things were unfamiliar and, perhaps, mysterious. Although our reception at the hands of the Tarahumaras could not have been more cordial and hospitable, lying unprotected in one's sleeping bag on the ground beneath cloud-filtered moonlight while listening to the distant—but very distinct—sounds of flute and pounding drums was not a situation designed to promote calmness. What could be more foreign to our ears than the sounds of Indians playing drums in a native beat?

We had no way of being certain that all the people in the community knew we were here; nor did we have any reason to believe we would be universally welcome. Tired as I was, my anxiety level was high and my sleep was dream-filled and fitful. The sound of the drums wavered between my consciousness and unconsciousness. When the first two men appeared in the night, and who turned out to be community criers announcing the upcoming Easter celebrations, I was quite startled. So was I immensely relieved when the purpose of their visit was explained.

So was I startled when the drunk man rode up on his horse. How do drunk Tarahumaras behave? Is he going to tell us we're not welcome? Is he enough in control of his horse that his horse won't step on us?

*Should we try to talk to him or simply ignore him and hope he will go away?*

*In spite of all the anxieties, however, there was something very pleasant about the strangeness of it all. In a way I cannot describe, even the music of a flute and drum was comforting.*

BERNARD L. FONTANA
*Field Diary*, March 22, 1978

WE HAD COME more than 300 miles by small plane from Tucson, Arizona, to see, hear, and sense one of the Tarahumaras' most important annual dance dramas. The occasion was Holy Week, or *Semana Santa* as it is called in Spanish. More precisely, the occasion was Holy Thursday, Good Friday, and Holy Saturday, Easter itself being reserved for the recovery of the participants. For the non-Christian or "pagan" Tarahumaras, who today are greatly in the minority, there are no such celebrations. But in attending one Tarahumara Easter celebration we could be fairly sure that at precisely the same time in dozens of other Tarahumara pueblos throughout the sierra very similar pageantry was taking place. Some would involve more people and be larger and more complex; others would involve fewer people and be greatly simplified. The outlines in all of them, however, would be the same.

The ceremonial year for Christianized Tarahumaras tends to be divided in terms of the kinds of musical instruments played at major church fiestas. The music of Easter, the time when fields are being prepared for planting, the time of spring and high hopes for a good yield of crops ahead, is the music of the drum and flute. The music of winter, with observances of the Feast of Our Lady of Guadalupe (December 12), Christmas, and the Feast of Epiphany (January 6), is that of violins, guitars, and rattles. The dancing of Easter is by men playing the role of Pharisees whose bodies are painted and some of whom wear feather headdresses. They are opposed by men who carry lances and bows and arrows. The dancing of winter is the dancing of matachines.

The common denominator of summer and winter church fiestas is tesgüino. In fact, it is the common denominator of all fiestas, church or otherwise. What connects the church fiestas of spring are the drum, flute, and Pharisee. What ties those of winter together are fiddle, guitar, and matachine. These same sets of dancers and musical instruments can be seen and heard at native yúmari and other feasts as well, with a rough division between spring-summer and fall-winter. Wendell Bennett has observed, "There is some overlapping, and at one curing *fiesta*, there were both *matachines* and *fariseos* [Pharisees] present. Much confusion resulted."

Is it possible, however, that Tarahumaras have unconsciously perceived their present world as divided into halves, one portion belonging to their own unbroken history and cultural continuum and the other belonging to the history of their contact with foreigners? Tarahumaras are a product of two worlds that have collided in them. They are corn, beans, and squash on one hand; goats, sheep, and cattle on the other. They have long known how to sew, but now they sew cloth manufactured by someone else. They have long known how to weave, but now they weave the wool of Spanish sheep. They drink tesgüino prepared in earthenware vessels; they drink Coca-Cola from king-size bottles. They continue to fashion their own dwellings, but now they use steel axes to accomplish the task.

Could it be that in their great church fiestas modern Tarahumaras have devised a way of dramatizing this reality of their lives? Does the Easter rite of spring belong to their native selves and the rites of winter to their new selves?

From place to place throughout the Sierra Tarahumara there is a great deal of variation in the ways in which these church fiestas are carried out. It is usual, for example, to see arches erected of tree limbs and flowers and branches to be used in Holy Week observances. We saw none where we were in 1978. And common in some areas is the *pascola* dancer who takes part in Holy Week and other spring and summer rituals. He does a fast-stepping dance while wearing strings of rattles wrapped around his ankles and lower legs and a belt around his waist with rattles attached. We saw none on the eastern side of the Continental Divide.

How long Tarahumaras have been involved in such church-oriented religious dance dramas is impossible to say. By 1717, Tarahumaras living in the mission settlement of San Francisco Satevó in eastern Tarahumara country had learned to play flageolets, bassoons, violins, harps, and an organ. For the most part, however, the historical record is mute on the subject of Tarahumara Christian religious fiestas.

In the early 1890s Carl Lumholtz witnessed such feasts, but he was inclined to dismiss them as being of little importance—probably because of his pro-native and anti-Mexican feelings. He wrote:

> I arrived in the pueblo on a Sunday, and a great many Indians had come in. Easter was approaching, and every Sunday during Lent, according to early missionaries' custom, the so-called "Pharisees" make their appearance. These are men who play an important part in the Easter festival, which always lasts several days. They paint their faces hideously, tog themselves up with feathers on their sombreros, and carry wooden swords painted with red figures. Such ceremonies were a clever device of the Jesuit and Franciscan missionaries to wean the Indians from their native feasts by offering them something equally attractive in the new religion they were teaching.

Easter ceremonies, like those of the winter season, have probably been going on in Tarahumara pueblos more or less continuously since the eighteenth century. In the 1890s there were secular (i.e., non-missionary) priests administering to Tarahumaras in at least two places in or near the eastern part of the sierra, at Norogachic and Nonoava, and a few new churches were built at the same time. With the return of the Jesuits to Tarahumara country as missionaries in 1900, church-related fiestas were probably given added impetus. Even so, Bennett remarked in the 1930s that ". . . it is the Indian himself who is now running the fiesta as a part of his culture, modifying the performance to suit his local requirements. Sometimes the *padre* appears . . . for a day or so once in two or three years; so the *fiestas* must be run by the Indians themselves."

It is probably this holding of religious observances without benefit of clergy that inspired a Lumholtz remark: "The feasts are still observed, while the teachings are forgotten." It is my impression that in many places the situation has changed little if at all since the days of Lumholtz or those of Bennett and Zingg.

Our arrival by small plane at the pueblo was a relatively unheralded event. One of us had met a Tarahumara woman from this place on the streets of Chihuahua City and had confirmed that the people were indeed going to have an Easter ceremony this year. She was left with the casual notice that the ceremony might have some visitors.

Where the plane landed was on a very short strip on a sloping summit above the settlement. Trees had been chopped out of the way and the larger boulders had been moved

aside to make it possible for a skilled pilot to land and take off again without getting killed. Fortunately, our pilot was skilled. The strip had been cleared for the Jesuits, some of whom get around in their mission area by small plane. It turned out, in fact, that a priest had been at the observances in Easter of the previous year.

Although we were not expected, we were met at the runway by a Tarahumara family: husband, wife, children, son-in-law, and grandchild. They simply happened to be there tending their flocks and looking after some burros. Following a few words of greeting and taking color pictures with a Polaroid camera and giving away the prints, we were helped by the family in gathering our gear together. Without any word or fanfare, they led us off on one of the narrow trails down the hill about a mile and a half away to the church. I struggled along with my weighty backpack, walking behind a boy about ten years old who had taken it upon himself to carry one of the heavy camera cases. He walked along as if he had no burden at all; I sweated my way down the path, hoping not to slip and make a fool of myself. Any more of a fool, that is, than I—and my friends— must already have seemed.

The church, as it turned out, was to be our home for the next four nights. We were escorted to an empty room in a structure built to the south of the church and abutting it, the convento. There were no questions asked of us. It was simply understood that this was where we were to stay.

We and our volunteer burden-bearers unloaded the gear and we were left to our own devices. Our room had a small wooden table, but it was otherwise bereft of furniture. We had a roof, four stone walls, a dirt floor, and a wooden door on pintles in a frame. The door could be closed. Our quarters were comfortable.

The church itself bore an inscription on the front with the date "1880." This is presumably when it was built. The nave and sanctuary were entirely of adobe; the façade was faced with cut stone; a handsome attached bell tower or *campanario* was built out of the same stone; rocks were piled to make an atrium wall. A roof of canoas lay over boards supported on long beams resting on wooden corbels protruding from the top of the nave walls. The church had a dirt floor and a choir loft that could be reached by climbing a wooden spiral stairway in the campanario. Except for simple altar furnishings and two bells that hung in the top of the campanario, the building contained no furniture.

The church stood in splendid isolation at the top of a small hill and at the base of another one rising behind it. It was at least 400 yards to the nearest household; most dwellings in the community were from a half-mile to two miles away. All the households were themselves several hundred yards from one another. It may be that the pueblo was defined as those houses *bajo la campana*, or "under the bell." Their residents could hear the tolling of the two great bells.

We spent our first late afternoon and evening visiting at some of the households. Our Polaroid camera and eagerness to trade yard goods for old clothing made us welcome, as well as the objects of considerable amusement. Embroidered clothing was exchanged for new muslin. We loitered in several yards and houses while people ground *esquiate* on metates, offered us tamales to eat, sewed, embroidered, and wove baskets. A man plowed his field with a pair of oxen; another carried fertilizer to his field.

During the night of our arrival there was a grand tesgüinada at one or two households. We had been invited to join in the fun, but as total strangers still unsure of ourselves, we politely declined. The next morning tesgüinada survivors lay in at least three yards, sound asleep under the warming sun.

Dreams of total isolation from the outside world vanished when we discovered that at least one family owned a battery-powered portable radio and liked to listen to popular Mexican music. An elaborate network of trails connected the pueblo to "civilization," and it was only about sixteen airline miles (or about twenty-five trail miles) from the nearest

Mexican town. People here were very cosmopolitan. All of them had been to Chihuahua City or to Juárez at one time or another, and a favorite theme in the graffiti carved into granaries and into the stone blocks of the church was buses and cars. There was even one graffito airplane.

Men, women, and children were going about the business of life as usual when we arrived on Tuesday of Holy Week. Even so, partly thanks to the sounds of the drum and flute, there was something of a festive air, the same sense of anticipation we have before Christmas or some similar religious holiday in our own culture. Women were using blue detergent to wash clothes in the creek, spreading them on nearby rocks and bushes to dry. People who lived in distant ranchos were coming to take part in the great celebration. They camped on hillsides just beyond the miles of stone walls marking individual and community lands. The campfires of these visitors glowed at night among the trees and rocks.

The two drummers who had visited us in our sleep on Tuesday night were dressed in white loincloths, printed blouses, white cotóns, and red headbands. One of them played a cane flute.

These drummers signaled the beginnings of Holy Week observances. They marched from household to household for miles around to announce that the celebration would begin at the church on Thursday. In more than one place they visited there was a tesgüinada in progress.

Wednesday was a time of rest, recovery, and further preparation for everyone. Drums and flutes could be heard throughout the day, even as we had heard them all during the night and would be hearing them until we left. In the morning a Tarahumara man

*The morning wait*

Tarahumara   III

rode up on horseback to our apartment by the church, dismounted, went into a small room next to ours that might be called a sacristy, and came out carrying two lances. He got back on his horse and rode off, taking the lances with him.

During the day two girls entered the church carrying buckets of water. They sprinkled the entire dirt floor, used homemade brooms to sweep it, and went away leaving the interior of the church spotless.

Except that the wind blew very hard, Wednesday night was without event. If there were tesgüinadas, no signs were evident.

About 11:00 A.M. on Holy Thursday a gray-haired man dressed in traditional costume came up to the church playing a drum and flute at the same time. He was the *kamporárero* (from the Spanish *tamborilero*, "drummer"). Shortly afterward, other men began to assemble. They included the local governors, the comisario ejidal, various officials whose titles we never learned, and assorted male onlookers. Nearly all of them were wearing freshly laundered loincloths, blouses, cotóns, and headbands, as well as truck tire-soled sandals and woolen sashes. A few wore Mexican straw hats and even fewer wore trousers and suit jackets over Mexican-style shirts. Two men were carrying wooden whirl rattles, something like the metal whirling rasps children in our own culture play at Halloween. These are called *matracas* in Spanish.

Something was about to happen; our level of anticipation rose. Moments later, we looked south across the plowed fields separating us from a row of hills. Six white-painted men walked quickly toward us. Two of them played drums as they moved along. They crossed an intervening stream and climbed the slope to a stone and wooden enclosure situated a short distance downhill from the church. The white-painted figures were the Pharisees; the enclosure was their dressing room and resting place.

No sooner had the Pharisees entered their enclosure than two soldiers, dressed smartly in traditional Tarahumara costume and carrying lances, strode up to the church. They were accompanied by the kamporárero and by a man dressed in black pants and black coat waving a red flag attached to a stick. The man with the red flag was the *capitán de los soldados* (captain of the soldiers), also called the *waru peshi* ("important man") or *bandedor* (flag waver). The soldiers stood at attention while the kamporárero made enough music for a whole orchestra and the waru peshi waved his red flag vigorously, no doubt exorcising whatever evil may have been present. All four soon marched off, drum and flute still playing and flag still waving.

There was a break in the action while more men, largely spectators, approached the church. A log was laid on the ground just south of the church, and some of the men—including the kamporárero, another drummer, the capitán de los soldados, and some distinguished-looking elders—sat on the log facing a clearing immediately to the east. This turned out to be the Pharisee dance plaza.

Just before noon someone climbed the bell tower and began to ring the bells. This was the signal to the Pharisees who had gathered in their enclosure to hurry up the hill to the front of the church while playing their drums. One of them had a guari basket on his head studded with wild turkey feathers and he carried a white flag on a stick. He was either a general or capitán of the Pharisees.

The torsos and legs of all the Pharisees were daubed with a white clay paint. Their blouses and cotóns were tied in bundles around their waists, the large part of the bundle at the back. Some of them carried wooden swords painted with various designs.

The entire group, sending dust flying into the air and creating a tremendous din with their drums, danced outside before disappearing into the church. They reemerged shortly, leaving four of their number to stand vigil by the altar at the entrance to the sanctuary.

Later, the Pharisees moved to the cleared area immediately east of where the kam-porárero, capitán de los soldados, and other officials were seated on the log, and began to dance to the accompaniment of the drum and flute music. A row of small rocks had been laid out in front of the log. At the end of each dance, a rock was rolled aside. Dancing continued until all the rocks were gone.

The dance itself consisted of Pharisees hurrying along in a kind of hop-and-skip, moving around and over the same two concentric oval circuits, single file. As each man passed the place where the officials were seated on the log, he would pivot and make a falsetto "woo-woo-woo" cry by slapping the fingers of one hand over his mouth. It was the very cry children in our own culture make when they imitate the "war whoops" of Indians.

The dancing lasted for about a half-hour. When it ended the perspiring Pharisees dashed helter-skelter down the hill to their enclosure.

While the dancing had been in progress, women and children had begun to gather, sitting down just outside the atrium wall on the south and east. They were dressed in their Easter best, brilliant red, orange, and green skirts, blouses, headbands, and shawls. Their feet were bare; a few wore cotóns. They were, to say the least, a riot of color. Whatever was drab in their surroundings was erased by their presence.

Soon the Pharisees returned to the atrium, dancing and playing their drums. All the women and children moved into the church, moving to the right side of the nave as they faced the altar. The Pharisees waited outside for a moment. While they were waiting a hapless dog came into the atrium, and one of the white-painted men sent him flying with his wooden sword. Tarahumaras, pastoralists that they are, have a special regard for dogs, but woe to the cur who gets underfoot on a ceremonial occasion!

Soldiers, spectators, and Pharisees moved in and out of the church. All this movement was preliminary to the grand procession. The capitán de los soldados came outside with his red flag and positioned himself in front of the lancers. He was followed immediately by three girls and a woman carrying two holy images from the altar, one of Our Lady of Guadalupe and the other of the Sacred Heart of Jesus (*Nuestra Señora de Guadalupe* and *Sagrado Corazón de Jesus* in Spanish). Both pictures, color lithographs, were framed. The girls and woman paused with the images almost as soon at they entered the atrium, and a fifth woman, holding the earthenware pottery censer that had been on the altar, censed both portraits with burning and sweet-smelling copal. This woman was the *moreami* (from the Tarahumara word *more*, "to offer incense"). Past middle age, she never smiled and clearly took her duties very seriously. Hers was a powerful presence.

The censing of the portraits was done in a carefully prescribed way. The moreami crossed herself several times in the sign of the cross and passed the burning incense before

*Tarahumara* 113

*Kamporárero, soldiers, and other celebrants*

114   Tarahumara

*The onlookers*

*Capitán de los soldados and his men*

116   Tarahumara

*Pharisee dance*

*A gathering in the church*

*Moreami censing the holy images*

each holy image nine times, pivoting after each three passes. While this took place, the rest of the people poured out of the church from their respective, segregated sides, the women from the north half of the nave and the men from the south half. The kamporárero and another soldier drummer played music at the same time, and the Pharisees came out of the church as well.

With the soldiers and the capitán de los soldados in the lead followed by the two holy pictures and the moreami, the entire procession—with possibly as many as 150 worshippers—moved slowly around the outside of the church and its attached wing in a counterclockwise path. There were seven pauses along the way during which the holy images received the smoke of incense. Some of the Pharisees danced along the route; two men kept matracas rasping their wooden sounds. This was pageantry at its peak.

Easter is the oldest celebration in Christendom. Holy Week is an expansion of Easter. It is a week meant to serve as a reminder of the passion, death, and resurrection of Christ. The whole story is symbolized in the *Via Dolorosa*, the Road of Sorrows or the Way of the Cross. The Via Dolorosa is the route in Jerusalem Christ is presumed to have followed carrying His cross to Mount Calvary. The major episodes are depicted in the fourteen Stations of the Cross seen in Catholic churches, usually in small paintings or as bas-relief sculptures. Sometimes fourteen plain, numbered crosses stand as symbols of the events. The first Station illustrates Jesus' condemnation to death. They continue with His journey to Calvary and the Crucifixion and conclude with the laying of His body in the tomb.

Had Tarahumaras known the liturgical requirements they might have paused fourteen times rather than seven. However, unknown to them, their procession was the Way of the Cross. They were commemorating events more than 2,000 years old which had taken place half the world removed from the Sierra Tarahumara. The pictures of Our Lady of Guadalupe and of the Sacred Heart of Jesus were Christ; the counterclockwise path around the church was the Via Dolorosa; the pauses were in memory of condemnation, agony, Crucifixion, and entombment; and by a series of almost mystical transformations, the Pharisees and soldiers who had been united at Jerusalem were no longer united, but appeared to be on opposing sides in the eternal war between good and evil.

Drums, flutes, wood rasps, church bells. White-painted bodies, lances, white flags, turkey feather headdresses, burning incense, red flag, loincloths, pleated skirts, babies wrapped in shawls. Plowed fields, full moon, blossoms on fruit trees, dogs, goats, sheep, horses, cows. The hope of spring. This was, after all, the Tarahumaras' own Via Dolorosa, their passion, their crucifixion, and, with luck, their resurrection. The casual observer may not recognize these transcendental truths through the Tarahumara disguise, but Christ, if He was watching, was probably pleased.

At the conclusion of the procession everyone crowded inside the church. The moreami chanted prayers, punctuated by mocking laughter from the Pharisees and the rattling of their wooden swords on the hardpacked earth floor. The smell of incense was overpowering. Copal has a pungent odor when it is burned. Two soldiers near the sanctuary carried bows and arrows. The holy pictures were replaced on the altar—Christ/Guadalupe to the tomb.

After leaving the church everyone convened just to the south, the women and children holding back along the south atrium wall. With the women clustered in one group, the Pharisees in another, the soldiers and male spectators in a third, and various other officials in a fourth, the community governor delivered a sermon in Tarahumara. We were told he was merely advising the people how they should behave, but he must have been doing it with humor. His remarks provoked much good-natured laughter among his congregation.

The conclusion of the sermon marked the end of the opening procession in the three-day observance. The women and children walked away from the church toward their respective households or camping places; one by one, the men, too, wandered off. The Pharisees went trooping over the countryside, pounding their drums and having a good time. By 1:30 P.M. it was over. The whole ceremony had taken only a little more than two hours. It had been so spectacular it had seemed much longer.

Almost precisely the same celebration took place that night, as soon as it got dark. A big bonfire was lighted near the dance plaza, so the whole scene was illuminated by firelight.

The Pharisees' dance was again followed by a grand procession with the two holy images from the church. And this time, while the procession was going on, four Pharisees, two with lances, stood vigil by the sanctuary.

By 10:00 P.M., the sermon and most of the people disappeared into the darkness of night. The candles were extinguished on the altar and the nave and sanctuary stood silent and black. The dying bonfire outside continued to offer a gentle light until after we had crawled into our bedrolls.

Shortly before 11:00 the next morning, the capitán de los soldados, the kamporár-ero, and six soldiers, including four lancers and two archers (carrying bows and arrows) came to the front of the church and repeated a version of the previous day's opening ceremony. They soon marched away and a group of Pharisees appeared. They were not, however, dancing or playing their drums. They had come to climb to the top of the church for the annual roof repair. The canoas forming the church roof were long and heavy, some of them possibly weighing as much as 250 pounds. A few were bug-eaten and rotten. A dozen or so Pharisees, white paint, turkey feather headdresses and all, threw the rotted timbers to the ground and picked up and moved those in good condition to new positions. It was obvious that Easter week was one of the few times of the year when this much manpower would be available. The Tarahumaras were taking advantage of it, and the white-painted men on the church may have been the most exotic-looking roof repair crew in the history of the New World.

The daytime dances and procession for Good Friday were essentially a carbon copy of those for Holy Thursday, except that the numbers of participants and Indian spectators seemed to grow. While the Pharisees were dancing in the clearing south of the church two Tarahumaras arrived with a pack horse. They had made a fifty-mile round trip to the nearest Mexican store and had returned with a crate of oranges and two cases of very warm king-size Coca-Cola. Pharisees and others took their turns buying the Cokes and fresh fruit. The Cokes were being sold for four pesos each, or eighteen cents a bottle! Even taking into account that the empty bottles had to be returned, eighteen cents for a

*A nighttime Pharisee dance*

Tarahumara

*A Pharisee roof repair crew*

*A straw Judas on the pole*

king-size Coke was less than it would have cost in Tucson, Arizona. Profit clearly was not the motive of the packers. They would make terrible capitalists.

During the Friday daylight procession, four soldiers, two of them with lances, stood vigil inside the church rather than Pharisees as had been the case the preceding day. Everything ended, as it had twice before, with a jocular sermon by the principal governor, and the men, women, and children again disappearing into the surrounding community and countryside.

We had expected a repeat performance for Friday night, but one of the elders hinted it was possible too many people had been drinking tesgüino, and the dances and procession would have to be canceled. We waited until long after dark, but by 9:00 P.M. we decided to go inside our room, close the door, and get some sleep.

It was almost as if closing the door had been the prearranged signal for the celebration to begin. Perhaps our hosts had been too polite to tell us they wanted to enjoy at least one series of dances and a procession without tourists. In any case, fifteen minutes after we were in our sleeping bags we heard drum and flute followed shortly by the banging of Pharisee drums, more than twenty of them. All this took place fewer than thirty yards from where we were lying. Too tired to get up to see what was happening, we could guess from the sounds, the smell of incense, and through our familiarity with the script.

Good Friday night's observances were much longer than the previous three, and they were marked by considerably more hilarity. A large group of men sat just outside our door and spent most of the night, or so it seemed to me, laughing. In a strange way I was transported to my childhood in northern California. I could remember falling asleep in my bed, warm and content beneath the covers, listening to the laughter of my parents and their friends as they played cards and listened to the radio in the living room. Far from keeping me awake, that happy laughter was the greatest reassurance a child could have that all was right with the world.

So it was with Good Friday night, 1978. I was warm and comfortable in my sleeping bag; just beyond the door were some of the happiest and most contented people in the world. Theirs was the gift of genuine laughter. I slept peacefully, waking once in awhile to smile myself back to sleep. The thundering of the drums, the laughter, and the incense were a lullaby.

Soon after awakening on Holy Saturday morning we learned the reason for the added length and hilarity of the ritual. A straw figure of Judas had been made the day before, and Judas, complete with a large wooden penis, had put in an appearance. We'll never know what went on with Judas until we return for another Good Friday night.

Tired out from what had been a many hours long celebration, and no doubt suffering from the effects of too much tesgüino as well, the participants in the grand Holy Saturday finale were later getting started. It was half past noon when the flag waving began. When the Pharisees made their appearance at the dance plaza, they had the straw figure of Judas with them. Two soldiers lashed Judas to a pole, then raised the pole with him on it, in the middle of the dance area. The dance of the Pharisees took place beneath him. A Pharisee wearing Bermuda shorts had glued a goat hair beard on his face, much to everyone's glee.

*The contemplator*

*A cruz mayor through the open door of a church*

As usual, the dancing was followed by the procession around the church with the two holy images. This time, however, when people left the nave the soldiers and Pharisees divided and ran two complete circuits around the church in opposite directions. They ended up at the dance plaza where Judas waited on his pole. The Pharisees rocked the pole back and forth until it toppled to the earth amid the laughter of onlookers. An elder stepped forward, untied the Judas figure, and carefully removed the straw from the clothes. The clothes—consisting of hat, shawl, neckerchief, sweater, and trousers—were saved. The straw and wooden penis were put to the torch and burned. Evil, if that is what Judas represented, had been dispatched.

Although we left after the burning of Judas, we were told that what would follow next would be informal wrestling matches between Tarahumara men and a night-long tesgüinada. Tarahumara wrestling consists of two opponents trying to be the first to get the other off his feet.

If this Easter celebration held true to form, the day of Easter itself was given over to holding trials for defendants accused of misdeeds, hearing disputes over inheritance, or tending to similar matters requiring the presence of the governor and his assistants. But our airplane safely left the short runway Saturday afternoon, and we were not there to see what happened the next day. It could only have been anticlimactic. The celebrants of the pueblo had already paid proper homage to spring. A good year seemed to be in the offing for those who live where night is the day of the moon.

# REFERENCE MATERIAL

# GLOSSARY

*atole:* cooked gruel made from corn that has been boiled several hours, drained, mashed, then boiled again.

*bandedor:* the "flag waver," or another name for the capitán de los soldados during Holy Week ceremonies; also waru peshi.

*barbecho:* the "moving corral" method of fertilizing fields.

*barranca:* a deep, wide canyon, less steep-sided and farther apart from rim to rim than implied in the Spanish concept cañon.

*basiáwi:* brome grass. The crushed, dried stem is used in fermenting sprouted corn to make tesgüino.

*betechi* or *beterachi:* a ranch, farm, or small farm.

*campanario:* a bell tower.

*canoas:* peeled, V-shaped logs with a continuous groove down their length, used for roofing.

*capitán de los soldados:* the "captain of the soldiers" during Holy Week ceremonies, also known as the waru peshi or bandedor.

*chapeón:* an overseer of the matachine dancers who is also the whip bearer.

*chicaton:* the Mayo Indian counterpart to the Tarahumara chapeón.

*chili piquín* or *chiltipín:* a particularly hot chili pepper which the Tarahumaras use.

*cilantro* or *culantro:* coriander, an Old World herb introduced by the conquistadors in the sixteenth century.

*comal:* a flat pottery griddle used to cook tortillas.

*comunidad:* a structure or open air site where Tarahumaras convene to discuss community matters.

*comisario ejidal:* the chief official of an ejidal.

*convento:* an addition to a church which serves as a sacristy and priest's quarters.

*corona:* the headdress worn by matachine dancers.

*cotón:* a poncho-like garment worn by men and women, made from coarse muslin, often embroidered.

*cuatro* or *dihibápa:* a game similar to quoits played with stone disks.

*dekóchi:* a granary or corn house.

*dowérami:* a team footrace in which a hoop is propelled along a course using a curved stick or dowéra.

*dutubúri:* a very fast dance performed by both men and women during curing fiestas.

*ejido:* a unit of land governed via the Mexican communal land system.

*esquiate:* cornmeal mush made by roasting corn and grinding it twice, the second time with water.

*galíki:* a house.

*guari:* a bowl-shaped twill plaited basket without a lid.

*kamporárero:* a musician who plays the drum and flute simultaneously.

*matachine:* the name given to certain dances probably of European origin which include violin and guitar accompaniment and elaborate costumes; the name given to the dancer of such a dance.

*matracas:* wooden whirl rattles used during fiestas.

*milpa:* slash and burn agriculture.

*monarco:* the lead dancer of a group of matachines.

*moreami:* the woman who censes the holy images as they are removed from the church on Holy Thursday.

*municipio:* a political subdivision in Mexico analogous to a county in the United States.

*nixtamal:* the dough for tortillas and tamales made by boiling corn with lime or ashes.

*olla:* large ceramic pottery jars, some capable of holding as much as fifty gallons.

*pascola:* a dancer who takes part in Holy Week and other spring and summer rituals.

*petaca:* a twill plaited lid-covered basket made in a single or double weave.

*petate:* a twill plaited mat used for sleeping.

*pinole:* cornmeal made by roasting corn in sand and grinding it twice.

*pueblo:* a modern Tarahumara settlement large enough to have a church and comunidad; not a multi-dwelling adobe structure.

*quelites:* potherbs collected in the wild and raised as garden crops, a staple in the Tarahumaras' diet.

*rancho:* a cluster of residences involving fewer households than a pueblo.

*rarahipa:* a kickball race run by Tarahumara men in relays, usually over a distance of two to twelve miles.

*reducción:* a mission village or pueblo into which the Tarahumaras were consolidated by the Jesuits in the sixteenth century.

*shaman:* a native priest with supernatural powers used in curing and controlling events.

*sikolí donéla:* small ceramic pots in which the starter for corn beer is prepared and left to ferment.

*tesgüinada:* a Tarahumara beer party.

*tesgüino* or *suguiki:* corn beer.

*trinchera:* rock-terraced slope.

*waru peshi:* literally "important man," the captain of the soldiers during Holy Week ceremonies, also known as the capitán de los soldados or bandedor.

*yerbero:* a Tarahumara who collects medicinal plants for market.

*yúmari:* a dance performed by the Tarahumara women accompanied by male chanters during curing fiestas.

# SELECTED BIBLIOGRAPHY

Given the very limited time we were able to spend in the Sierra Tarahumara, we have drawn heavily on the hard work and published efforts of many people who were there ahead of us. The "basic" list consists of the books most often consulted. The "secondary" list includes books and articles consulted less often but from which quotations have been made or other references drawn.

BASIC.

BENNETT, WENDELL C., and ROBERT M. ZINGG
   1976   *The Tarahumara: an Indian tribe in northern Mexico.* Glorieta, New Mexico, The Rio Grande Press, Inc. [This is a reprint of the 1935 University of Chicago edition, with a new introduction and the addition of 96 color plates.]

BYE, ROBERT A., JR.
   1976   "Ethnoecology of the Tarahumara of Chihuahua, Mexico." Unpublished Ph.D. thesis, Department of Biology, Harvard University, Cambridge, Massachusetts.

DUNNE, PETER M.
   1948   *Early Jesuit missions in Tarahumara.* Berkeley and Los Angeles, University of California Press.

KENNEDY, JOHN G.
   1978   *Tarahumara of the Sierra Madre: beer, ecology, and social organization.* Arlington Heights, Illinois, AHM Publishing Corporation.

LUMHOLTZ, CARL
   1973   *Unknown Mexico. A record of five years' exploration among the tribes of the western Sierra Madre; in the Tierra Caliente of Tepic and Jalisco; and among*

*the Tarascos of Michoacan.* Glorieta, New Mexico, the Rio Grande Press. [The most recent reprint of a two-volume work first published in 1902.]

PENNINGTON, CAMPBELL W.

1963    *The Tarahumar of Mexico.* Salt Lake City, University of Utah Press.


SECONDARY.

ABBEY, EDWARD

1975    A tale of the Sierra Madre. *Mountain Gazette,* no. 35 (July), pp. 10–17. Denver, Write On Publishing House, Inc.

ANONYMOUS

1927    The Nurmis of Mexico. *Literary Digest,* Vol. 92, no. 1 (January 1), p. 47. New York, Funk and Wagnalls Company.

ARCHIBALD, ROBERT

1978    Indian labor at the California missions: slavery or salvation? *Journal of San Diego History,* Vol. 24, no. 2 (Spring), pp. 172–82. San Diego, San Diego Historical Society.

ARTAUD, ANTONIN

1976    *The peyote dance.* Translated from the French by Helen Weaver. New York, Farrar, Straus, and Giroux.

BALKE, BRUNO, and CLYDE SNOW

1965    Anthropological and physiological observations on Tarahumara endurance runners. *American Journal of Physical Anthropology,* Vol. 23, no. 3 (September), pp. 293–301. Philadelphia, Wistar Institute of Anatomy and Biology.

BASAURI, CARLOS

1929    *Monografía de los Tarahumaras.* México, Talleres Gráficos de la Nación.

CHAMPION, J, R.

1955    Acculturation among the Tarahumara of northwest Mexico since 1890. *Transactions of the New York Academy of Sciences,* series 2, Vol. 17, no. 7 (May), pp. 560–66. New York.

CLEGG, REED S.

1972    Tarahumara Indians. *Rocky Mountain Medical Journal,* Vol. 69, no. 1 (January), pp. 57–58. Denver, Colorado Medical Society.

ESCALONA, JOSEPH DE

1744    [A report written June 7, 1744, from the mission station of Santissimo Nombre de María de Sisoguichic.] Original on file in the Bancroft Library, University of California, Berkeley, California. Mexican Manuscript (M-M) 1716, no. 19.

FERNANDEZ DE ABEE, JUAN Y.

1744    [A report written July 8, 1744, from the mission station of Jesús Carichíc.]

Original on file in the Bancroft Library, University of California, Berkeley, California. Mexican Manuscript (M-M) 1716, no. 21.

FONTANA, BERNARD L.; EDMOND J. B. FAUBERT and BARNEY T. BURNS
1977    *The other Southwest. Indian arts and crafts of northwestern Mexico.* Phoenix, The Heard Museum.

FRIED, JACOB
1969    The Tarahumara. In *Handbook of Middle American Indians,* edited by Robert Wauchope, Vol. 8, *Ethnology,* part 2, edited by Evon Z. Vogt, pp. 846–70. Austin, University of Texas Press.

GAJDUSEK, D. CARLETON
1953    The Sierra Tarahumara. *The Geographical Review,* Vol. 43, pp. 15–38. New York, American Geographical Society.

GREEN, JUDITH S.
1971    Archaeological Chihuahuan textiles and modern Tarahumara weaving. *Ethnos,* Vol. 36, pp. 115–30. Stockholm, National Museum of Ethnography.

GROOM, DALE
1971    Cardiovascular observations on Tarahumara Indian runners—the modern Spartans. *American Heart Journal,* Vol. 81, no. 3 (March), pp. 304–14. St. Louis, C. V. Mosby Company.

JENKINSON, MICHAEL
1972    The glory of the long-distance runner. *Natural History,* Vol. 81, no. 1 (January), pp. 54–65. New York, American Museum of Natural History.

LUMHOLTZ, CARL
1894    Tarahumari life and customs. *Scribner's Magazine,* Vol. 16, no. 9 (September), pp. 296–311. New York, Charles Scribner's Sons.

OCAMPO, MANUEL
1950    *Historia de la misión de la Tarahumara, 1900–1950.* México, Editorial "Buena Prensa."

PLANCARTE, FRANCISCO M.
1954    El problema indígena Tarahumara. *Memorias del Instituto Nacional Indigenista,* no. 5. México.

SCHMIDT, ROBERT H.
1973    A geographical survey of Chihuahua. *Southwestern Studies Monograph,* no. 37. El Paso, Texas Western Press.

SCHWATKA, FREDERICK
1892    Land of the living cliff dwellers. *The Century Magazine,* Vol. 44, no. 2 (June), pp. 271–76. New York, The Century Company; London, T. Fisher Unwin.
1977    *In the land of cave and cliff dwellers.* Glorieta, New Mexico, The Rio Grande Press. [Reprint of the 1893 original.]

SHEPHERD, GRANT
    1938    *The silver magnet. Fifty years in a Mexican silver mine.* New York, E. P. Dutton and Company, Inc.

SHRAKE, EDWIN
    1967    A lonely tribe of long-distance runners. *Sports Illustrated,* Vol. 26, no. 2 (January), pp. 56–62, 65–67. Chicago, Time, Inc.

THORD-GRAY, I.
    1955    *Tarahumara-English, English-Tarahumara dictionary.* Coral Gables, Florida, University of Miami Press.

TISDALE, FREDERICK
    1928    The greatest long-distance runners in the world. *The Mentor,* Vol. 16, No. 2 (March), pp. 19–20. Springfield, Ohio, Crowell Publishing Company.

ZINGG, ROBERT M.
    1938    Christmasing with the Tarahumaras. In *Coyote wisdom,* edited by J. Frank Dobie, Mody C. Boatright, and Harry H. Ransom, pp. 207–24. *Texas Folklore Society Publications,* no. 14. Austin.

# INDEX

Faubert, Edmond J. B., xi, xvi
Fernández de Abee, Juan Ysidro, S.J., 25; quoted, 1, 7–8, 9, 14, 16, 57
Ferrocarril Chihuahua al Pacífico, 6, 18
Fontana, Hazel M., xi
Fonte, Juan, S.J., 8, 13, 16, 40
forestry, 6, 18, 19, 79
Franciscans, 14–15, 66, 107. *See also* Tarahumara Indians, religion

Gonzáles, Carmen, xi
granaries, 26, 29. *See also* Tarahumara Indians, storage
Grand Canyon, Arizona, 6
Guadalupe, Feast of, 14, 96, 106
Guadiana, Nueva Vizcaya, 8
Guazapar Indians, 9
Guazapares, Chihuahua, 90

Hidalgo del Parral, Chihuahua, xv, 9, 12, 13
Holy Week, 14, 19, 106–7, 110, 112–13, 120, 121, 125, 128. *See also* Easter
hospitals, 15, 19, 21, 25. *See also* Tarahumara Indians, medical care
Huejotitlán. *See* San Gerónimo de Huejotitlán, Chihuahua

Jesuits, xvi, 6, 8, 9, 14–15, 19, 25, 26, 47, 49, 66, 102, 107, 108. *See also* Tarahumara Indians, religion
Jesús Carichíc. *See* Carichíc
Juárez, Chihuahua, 55, 110
Judas, 125, 128

Kennedy, John G., 24, 34, 46, 54; quoted, 19, 50

Law of Colonization, 15
Los Angeles, 19
lumber. *See* forestry
Lumholtz, Carl S., 23–24, 25, 40, 51, 90, 108; quoted, 18, 23, 49–50, 63, 75, 88, 107–8

Mátachic, Chihuahua, 12
*matachines*, 51, 95–96, 99, 102, 106. *See also* Tarahumara Indians, dancing
Mayo Indians, 38, 99
Merrill, William, xi
Mexico City, 92
mining, 9, 12, 13, 18
missionaries. *See* Franciscans; Jesuits
missions. *See* churches
Murphey, Helen, xi
musical instruments, 14, 35, 107, 110, 112, 125. *See also* Tarahumara Indians, music

Nabogame, Chihuahua, 15
Navajoland, 4
Nonoava, Chihuahua, 1, 12, 107
Norogachic, Chihuahua, 1, 12, 107
Nueva Vizcaya, New Spain, 12, 14

Ojinago, Chihuahua, 18

Pachuca, Hidalgo, 92
Palmer, Edward, 24
Pamachic, Chihuahua, 1
Papago Indians, 38
Papigochic, Chihuahua, 12, 13. *See also* Río Papagochic
Parral, Chihuahua. *See* Hidalgo del Parral, Chihuahua
peyote, 55–56
Pharisees, 51, 106, 107, 112–13, 120, 121, 125, 128
Pima Indians, 38
Piman language, 38
Polaroid Corporation, xi
Polaroid SX-70 camera, xi, 108, 109
pottery, 32, 48, 81, 92, 94. *See also* Tarahumara Indians, pottery making
Presidio, Texas, 18
Pueblo Indians, 4, 96

rainfall, 27
Rarámuri, xi, 26, 54; defined, xv, 86. *See also* Tarahumara Indians
*reducción*, 8, 9, 25
reduction. *See reducción*
Río Balleza, 9
Río Batopilas, 1, 6, 24. *See also* Batopilas, Chihuahua
Río Bravo, xv
Río Conchos, 9, 12
Rio Grande, xv
Rio Grande Press (New Mexico), 24
Río Papigochic, 9, 12, 13. *See also* Papigochic, Chihuahua
Río San Ignacio, 12
Río San Pedro, 9
Río Urique, 1, 6, 31
Río Verde, 1, 6
Russell, Alexander, Jr., xi, xvi
Russell, Jean, xi

San Antonio, Texas, 92
San Bernabé Cusihuiriachic. *See* Cusihuiriachic, Chihuahua
San Borja, Chihuahua, 1
San Felipe de Conchos, 9
San Francisco Satevó, Chihuahua, 107
San Gabriel, Chihuahua, 9

## ABOUT THE AUTHOR

Bernard L. Fontana is a retired field historian for the University of Arizona. He has published several works on southwestern Indian life and Spanish influences. Since 1956, he and his family have lived on land adjacent to the San Xavier (Tohono O'odham) Indian Reservation in Tucson, Arizona. Fontana has also done extensive archaeological and historical research on Mission San Xavier del Bac.

## ABOUT THE PHOTOGRAPHER

John P. Schaefer is past president of the University of Arizona and an accomplished photographer of the West. Along with Bernard L. Fontana, Schaefer became interested in the people, culture, and crafts of the Tarahumara. In addition to photographing and writing about the Tarahumara, he and Fontana collected artifacts of Tarahumara material culture for a major exhibit at the Arizona State Museum.